The Business of Cou

ISBN-13: 978-1547065936

ISBN-10: 1547065931

First published 2017

CONTENTS

Introduction:

Few people grow up with a burning ambition to become a professional counsellor. More commonly an interest in counselling is germinated over a long period of time, perhaps triggered by experiencing counselling first hand, or by a desire to understand ourselves better, or driven by an altruistic nature to help others. Many new therapists enter the profession later in life, as a second career, with mortgages, children and relationships in tow.

Training to become a counsellor is hard work. And expensive. It means re-entering the classroom, requires dedication to hours and hours of study, ploughing through academic literature, undertaking considerable personal therapy, racking up client hours (usually done for free), and supervision (usually done for a fee). And by the time we've learnt the basic skills, techniques and theories, we realise that we have only just begun.

The training, if done right, can prepare us for the profession of counselling. But little or no attention is given to **the Business of Counselling**. While we might have set out with the original intention of putting the daily commute behind us and becoming a private practitioner perhaps working from a spare room at home or in a setting we care about, we find that turning this ambition into reality is fraught with challenges that few know how to overcome. Setting up a business. Finding premises. Marketing a service. Taking money. Paying tax. Monitoring contacts. Issuing and chasing invoices. Organising liability insurances. The list goes on.

Earning money in the UK is still predominantly focused on working for a company as an employee, doing a specific job and getting paid at the end of the month directly into our bank account, with taxes deducted under the "pay as you earn" (PAYE) scheme. Employers are obliged to give paid holiday, pension contributions, health benefits etc., and we have colleagues to work and socialise with, and a place to go to (and leave from) work.

Being an employee also means focusing on just one aspect of that business. A member of the accounts team has little experience of what the sales team do, and the sales team little experience of the operations team. Running your own business means developing a suite of skills that enable you to control *all* aspects of your business, and not having anyone else to turn to for advice. Pretty daunting for the uninitiated.

No surprise, then, that most people choose, consciously or unconsciously, to put up with commuting and office politics, and work for an employer, remaining in the sheltered comfort of an environment that they naively believe gives them security.

What they fail to see is that this "security" is actually little more than ignorance to the true state of the business or the true intensions of the business owner/shareholders, and that all the time they remain in the deluded comfort zone of a "secure" job, they are not pushing themselves to develop the skills that would set them free to become entrepreneurs in their own right.

This book, and the workshops, resources and coaching services that accompany it, is designed to help you overcome these barriers and turn your counselling skills into a successful business. You may never become financially wealthy as a therapist - after all, there are only so many hours in a week - but there is no reason why you cannot earn a respectable living from being a professional counsellor by embracing **the business of counselling**.

Over the coming chapters, we hope to bring our own experiences in creating successful private practices. Our aim is to keep it simple, explain things in non-technical language, and *gently* guide you through the common hesitancies that stop so many great counsellors from making their skills available to a needy audience.

We bring combined experience in sales, marketing, business management, coaching and human resource management, skills that proved invaluable to us in our approach to setting up our own practices. We will use these skills to guide you through the processes of conquering the mental barriers you face, show you how to "sell" your service in today's modern consumer environment, and how to stand out from the crowd. Then we will help you set up your practice with checklists and templates for administrating your business, as well as tips and tricks learned from our own experience.

We begin by asking **What's stopping you?!**, examining the mental and emotional barriers that slow us down and stop us from succeeding with ventures that take us out of our comfort zones. Then in Section 2 we look at the **Essential Marketing Essentials** needed to ensure you develop a marketing strategy that works and does not cost a fortune. In Section 3, we look at the **Accounting Basics** needed to ensure you manage and track client takings, how much they owe you and how much they have paid you. Here we will introduce suggested systems to manage your money, keep track of income and expenditure, and keep the Tax Man happy with clear records. Finally in Section 4 we look at the **Practice Management Systems** that will enable you to drive efficiency and effectiveness into your practice, help keep you safe, and help you incrementally improve your service so that new clients increasingly come through referrals from happy clients and suitably impressed colleagues.

Lets begin!

Actually, just before we get going, there is one other thing that is important to consider. Ethics. Specifically the ethics of making money whilst seeking to help others with their emotional and mental health issues. These are uncomfortable bedfellows. Therapists have a tendency to make everything "about the client", declaring actions in terms of projections or transferences. The bottom line is this – it is reasonable to make a reasonable living from providing a reasonable service to help people. You are trading your time and skills to help others in the same way a plumber or a dentist or a shopkeeper does. Only you, the individual therapist, will know whether your intent is true – exploitation is possible in almost any trade. An old boss of mine once wagged his finger at a journalist in a sage like manner and said, "a clear conscience is the softest pillow!" I prefer to sleep well at night.

It is somewhat inevitable that you will receive criticism from clients with whom you struggle to help. Indeed, it is somewhat inevitable that there will be criticism of this book – teaching people how to turn counselling into a business appears, at one level, to be exploitative. In the last section of the book, we provide means by which you can measure the performance of your client work. So if you see a dip in progress with a client, discuss it with them and with your supervisor, and be ready to let that client go, or better still, make a good referral so that your client can continue to make progress elsewhere. Don't let your personal need – or greed – give you sleepless nights.

OK. Now let's get going.

Section 1 - What's stopping you?!

Practical questions vs. mental attitude

Starting any new venture brings up a wide range of practical questions. Where should I practice? How do I find premises? Do I need a business bank account? Do I need an accountant? How much should I pay for a website? The list grows and grows, and goes on to become quite daunting.

This is exacerbated by the constant bombardment from other business providers. When that local magazine calls and offers you a too-good-to-miss-deal for an advert (which they will happily create for you) for a local magazine which they tell you is read by thousands of people, do you write that cheque for £700 or not?

Or when the website provider tells you that you're missing out on potential customers because your website is "not optimised for search engines", do you respond to their criticism and buy an optimisation service? Do you even understand what they mean?!

This FUD (Fear, Uncertainty and Doubt) technique was first coined by an ex-employee of a large computer manufacturer. He realised that this computer manufacturers' sales people used FUD to discredit the growing number of competitors, and would ask questions like "would you really trust a small computer company with such a vital business operation?" The aim was to simply play on the buyers' fears and uncertainties by deliberately introducing doubt.

While all of your practical questions need to be answered, the truth is that the real battle is not one of knowledge – the real battle is one of mental attitude. If you are able to progress *despite* your own fears, uncertainties and doubts, you will be able to find answers to any practical question that you might have. There are a number of factors that make this the greatest challenge.

Principal among those challenges is our characteristics. Good therapists possess the many "soft" skills required to develop relationship, empathy, patience. Therapists, by their very nature, do not necessarily make great hard hitting Chief Executives, target driven Sales Directors, or cut throat entrepreneurs. We therapists are *naturally biased* towards having those skills required to be great therapists, and not *naturally biased* towards being clear thinking business people. That is not to say that they are mutually exclusive – it is entirely possible for us to learn other skills – and this is what this book is designed to help you do, but cut yourself some slack if you feel inadequate as a business person – you're a therapist, and you possess skills that many business people lack.

Over the years, psychologists seeking to understand human psychology better have developed many psychometric tests designed to measure suitability of individuals for specific tasks. These tests, first developed by the US army, have been funded and developed by organisations that have sought to select individuals with specific traits for specific job roles. While no one test can really pigeonhole any individual into a fixed profile, there are surprising general traits amongst the groupings. The same traits that bias us to be great therapists are the same traits that see us working in Human Resource departments, nursing, teaching, humanitarian work or training. We're good at those roles because those roles fit our *naturally biased* characteristics. But to be a successful private practitioner, we may well have to learn skills that take us outside of our natural bias, and this is hard work.

Throughout our schooling we learn "by rote", being spoon-fed knowledge that we are told that we must learn. What we are not often encouraged to do is "learn by discovery", experimenting and acquiring knowledge through trail and error. Our conservative culture cautions us to remain well within safe limits. Our risk-averse, safety-first society wants to blame those who get things wrong. All this creates a fear of failure. We fear being ridiculed or ostracized if we get something wrong. And this fear paralyses us from even trying.

As you proceed through the other sections of this book, we hope to answer some of the bigger practical questions that you have about setting up in private practice, but this section focuses on tuning your mind towards creating a can-do mind set designed to equip you to achieve success. Overcoming your own fears, uncertainties and doubts will mean that you will be able to find the answers to all your questions, by not being afraid to ask the right people or experiment. Indeed, this book will not give you a prescriptive list of what you should and should not do, rather it will provoke thought and share experience to encourage you to consider how you might solve your own problems in your own way.

Overcoming barriers to setting up in private practice:

What stops us from achieving anything in life? What stops us from training for a marathon, or running for parliament, or dieting, or writing that book? What motivates those who get up at the crack of dawn to run 4 miles before breakfast, or those who sit and meditate before starting their day in the quiet and cool of the morning? What is it that marks "successful" people apart from those who seem to drift through life, only ever glimpsing a mere vision of their actual potential?

Some people believe that these individuals are lucky, that perhaps they are naturally skilled athletically, or have an intellect that lends itself to business, or that they were perhaps born into wealth that meant they were able to have an easy time of playing at business until they made it themselves.

The truth is very different. The truth is that these successful people have developed a mind-set, a way of continually challenging themselves, of being prepared to take calculated risk. Successful people have developed a spirit of curiosity, minds that want to solve problems by asking "how" and "why".

The difference between those that succeed and those that fail is that the "succeeders" do not let their many failures stop them from trying again and again. Things in life go wrong, regardless of who you are. Whenever things go wrong in our lives we have three possible ways of reacting. We can choose to blame ourselves. We can choose to blame anyone and anything except ourselves.

Or we can choose to learn from our experiences and seek to overcome.

If we approach these moments in our lives with curious contemplation, if we allow ourselves to engage with the pain of the past and sit through the fear of these moments and understand what lessons we can learn from each knock-back, we can turn them into powerful moments of transformation.

Think of it like this. Cast your mind back to mathematics class in school. Do you recall sitting in classes and being presented with something like this:

$$\text{Solve x for the following:} \quad x^2 - 5x + 4 = 0$$

This is an algebraic equation. Don't worry - I'm not expecting you to solve it[1], but I would like you to recall your experience of having to solve such equations. Some of my classmates would race each other to be the quickest to finish. Others would simply stare at the blackboard, overwhelmed with where to start, and then copy the person next to them! But none of them, as far as I know, have ever had to actually used this knowledge in their working lives - as soon as the module is complete, algebra gets pushed to the vault of nostalgic memories from the past.

So why do we learn algebra at all? Why do we put our children through this ordeal?! What are we seeking to teach them? We could answer this by saying that we set our children problems to solve, including algebraic equations, because we want them to learn to approach problems in life with analysis and determination, not defeat and resignation.

---

[1] *The answer, in case you wondered, is 4*

This is counter-intuitive. As humans, we are pain averse. Most of us shrink from pain, much like we perhaps shrank from the pain of algebraic equations. But if we learn to approach life's problems as a riddle to be solved, then we build a resilience that can help us throughout life.

My mother, like mothers all over the world, did her utmost to keep me from pain. When I was a child, she moved small items away from my reach to prevent me from putting them into my mouth and choking. She kept me out of my fathers' toolbox so as to prevent me from hurting myself as I tried to mimic him. And she would watch me from the kitchen window while I played, one eye on the dinner cooking on the stove, and one eye on me. Thank God for mothers! Yet it is in falling over that we learn to walk; it was through my parents' example, encouragement and gentle instruction that I learned to talk; through their example and their discipline that I was taught their version of right and wrong. All learning, all play, all discovery is about balancing the risk of being hurt with the desire to discover. The good enough parent will let the child fall, will let the child experience frustration, will let them discover for themselves that horseradish is hot, all the time balancing the risk of real injury with the need to let them learn.

This is the essence of play, and the essence of learning. This is the essence of success in life. It is through pain that we learn. Without pain, we struggle to learn. If we fail to learn from past pain, we develop phobias and shrink back from life out of fear of further pain.

This shrinking back is given away in a persons script – one way or another, they are continually reminding themselves that they "can't". They "can't" run. They "can't" afford the time in their busy schedules. They "can't" do maths.

The problem is that if you have grown up suspicious of the world and over-cautious in your adventurous play, if you have spent much of your life telling yourself that you "can't", then:

a. you're unlikely to really try to overcome barriers and strive to achieve, preferring instead to *stay within the comfortable limits of familiarity*

b. you're *expecting to have these suspicions confirmed* so the moment that first hurdle appears, the moment you've been telling yourself to expect, you've already been defeated by it.

When I met my personal trainer in 2012, he started by telling me a mantra that he'd learned during his time as a Royal Marine Commando - "It's a state of mind," he told me, a strap line used in Royal Marine advertising campaigns. This was an epiphany - I suddenly realised how often I told myself that "I am unfit", that "I am fat", that "I can't run" (and that "I have never been able to run"), that "I don't like press-ups", that "I am concerned about catching a cold by being outdoors", and that "I am ashamed of how my 40-something physique would look in front of others (who I presumed would all much fitter than me) in the training group".

For me to overcome my life-long block of wanting-to-get-fit-and-loose-weight-but-never-having-the-motivation-to-do-so would mean me embodying this mantra - in short, it meant that I would have to coach myself, push myself to break my own "can't's" and not let a mental attitude that had dogged me for twenty years to dog me for one moment longer! Like Roy Castle sang in the theme tune from the 80's TV show Record Breakers, "If you want to be the best, if you want to beat the rest, dedication is what you need".

Dedication means not giving up. It means pushing yourself to achieve slightly more than your previous best. It means acquiring new skills and learning new methods whenever you reach the limit of your current knowledge. It means doing it again and again and again until (a) you get it right and (b) you no longer fear getting it wrong because you know you *can* get it right.

The truth is that in practice I continually have to fight with myself, push myself, remind myself of my preference for cake and TV, and seek to replace them with yet more determination. I still suffer bouts of self-doubt, moments of fearful self-consciousness and days when I lack motivation. But I am getting better all the time at recovering from these set backs. Two steps forward, one step back.

Being successful at any pursuit - including setting up a private practice - requires that we overcome the barriers we ourselves place in our way.

In this chapter, we want to challenge you to think about the things you do and say to yourself that stop you from achieving all you can achieve. We will try to answer some of the more specific barriers that counsellors face, before going on to suggest a step-by-step guide for building a private practice.

Much has been written and taught about motivation, but no amount of reading or guides or gurus can make you let go of negative attitudes towards becoming successful - only you can do that.

Thinking like an Entrepreneur

Entrepreneurs are often thought to be inventive, fearless risk-takers. But the truth is that entrepreneurs are inventive, calculated risk-takers who do not allow fear to stop them from trying. And by taking calculated risks, they are able to try their inventiveness to exploit niches and sell products where others have not. It is this inventiveness, and they way that they de-risk their enterprises that is the essence of what we can learn from the entrepreneur.

Characteristic 1 – "How could this be done better?"

The first thing we can notice from the entrepreneur is the way in which they look at an existing business or idea and ask themselves "could this be done better?" They are hungry consumers and avid observers that allow themselves to experience products and services, leaving their natural curiosity to wonder about ways things could be done better.

For counsellors, this might mean looking at a competitors website, their brochures, their facilities. It might mean integrating our own experiences as clients in therapy and allowing ourselves to note what we liked and disliked, what felt was good or professional, or what we felt was poor or off-putting. It might mean working with your supervisor and talking to them about their experiences.

This information then leads us to think about what sort of service we would like to offer. What would you want potential clients to think when they visit your website, when they visit your premises, when they read you literature, when they meet you, when they get your business card?

In Section 2 – Essential marketing essentials – we will take this way of thinking and use it to help you create your own individual identity as a counsellor.

Characteristic 2 – "Curiosity"

The next important characteristic of the entrepreneur is the way in which they ask "how" and "why" in order to overcome barriers. They are inquisitive and use the answers they get to plug knowledge in their own understanding, to discover how things are done before going ahead and taking unnecessary risks.

Think about the toddler. We have probably all met children at that wonderful stage in life where they ask "why" about almost everything. This curiosity is an important part of a child's development, creating links between different bits of knowledge until they form an understanding of the world around them.

This child-like attitude of mind to discovery is a key characteristic of the entrepreneur. They use it in the same way as the inquisitive toddler – to plug gaps in their understanding, to link different bits of information together.

What does this mean practically? It means that if they do not understand how websites work, they go and find out, conducting research and asking questions of people who do know. It means that if they do not understand how to advertise a product, they go and find out, conducting research and asking questions of people who do know.

By doing this, they de-risk their business. Their willingness to learn means that they can understand what could go wrong, how to avoid costly mistakes, how to leverage someone else's experience to remove the risk of doing it wrong.

Indeed, seeing as you're reading this, you're already emulating this characteristic!

There are always things that we do not know. Even the brightest minds have gaps in their knowledge. The big difference is that rather than throwing their arms in the air and giving up, entrepreneurial mind adopts an inquisitive stance, is not afraid to ask questions, and is prepared to ponder problems without loosing hope of them being solved.

In the Workshop A, you will begin to list the gaps in your knowledge. But rather than being daunted by the length and complexity of your list, allow yourself to think like an entrepreneur and slowly plug the gaps in your knowledge, de-risk your venture, and discover that you are just as capable as anyone in achieving success.

Characteristic 3 – "I use my fear to inform me"

In a similar way, entrepreneurs are not put-off by fear. Instead, they use their fear to inform them of risks and threats to their enterprise, helping them to de-risk what they are doing by exposing areas where care needs to be taken.

Unfortunately, most of us suffer a degree of paralysis through fear. The playground taught us to avoid the ridicule of our peers by not making fools of ourselves. Our "safety-first" culture has created a blame environment where mistakes are not tolerated. Our schools spoon-feed us knowledge, rather than encouraging us to discover for ourselves. And our media, with its reports of all the bad things that could possibly go wrong for us in this world, keep us firmly sat on our sofas staring at TVs for "entertainment".

The entrepreneur is able to avoid being paralysed by fear by manipulating this emotion to instead benefit them. They have taught themselves that fear is information to be respected, and it leads them to ask questions that help them remove reckless risk from their venture.

Let's look at how the entrepreneur might respond to a phone call from a magazine selling advertising space. The entrepreneur first separates out the fear of not having enough new clients (the FUD[2] injected by the sales person) and understands that the fear is really about spending money on something that is unproven.

---

[2] *FUD – Fear, Uncertainty and Doubt*

Then they will start asking questions. What is the age and gender profile of the reader? Where is the magazine distributed? How is the magazine distributed? Can the magazine show me circulation figures? Does the magazine have any success stories that prove a return on investment for the advertiser? Can I get copies of past magazines to look at so I can see the quality of the publication and the type of business that is also advertising?

Then they will start asking questions of themselves. Do I really understand the mechanics of what makes a successful advert? Does the circulation data provided match the profile of the individual I'm seeking to reach with my business? Can I call up some of these other businesses and ask them how successful the advertising has been for them.

Rather than being paralysed by fear, they are informed by it and can make an informed decision about whether the £700 is likely to result in £700-plus in return.

Characteristic 4 – "I learn by trying"

The single biggest barrier to achieving anything is in the failure to act or *do*. We are so used to being able to have what we want without too much discomfort that we want success without too much effort, too. We want gratification quickly. Our children want to be pop stars or footballers, not engineers or scientists.

Those individuals who succeed have often had to overcome difficulty in their own lives. They have been burnt by the fires of failure, they have suffered the torment of having nothing, and they have lived through the destruction of a Hamlet-like indecision. This failure is the refiners fire, the alchemists *vas* in which these individuals have been changed from base metal into gold. The fires in their lives leave them with a determination that cannot be broken. They are not born this way. They are not lucky. They are not privileged. They are human like you and me. But the experiences of their lives has led them to this fundamental conclusion: do something.

Action, not questioning. Action, not planning. Action, not dreaming about what might be if only someone would come and do it for them. They don't always head off in exactly the right direction, but they do set off. Instead of staring out into the distance to try and spot the very best path, the path with the least stumbling blocks, they instead head off in what they quickly determine is roughly the right direction, and then they overcome obstacles as they come across them, and make necessary adjustments on the road as required in order for them to reach their goal.

It is far more important to develop the attitude of *doing* vs. developing the skills of planning; far better to learn about business while you're running a business vs. going to college to get a degree that tells you how to run a business but does not give you any practical experience. Or experimenting with the different foods and diets until you find one that works for you vs. asking the nutritionist to tell you what to eat. Training is partially important, but with the attitude of *doing*, you'll learn everything you need anyway.

Doing something – doing anything – is more important than doing nothing. Doing something and getting it wrong is better than doing nothing and fretting about the right way or the best way or the most efficient way of achieving a goal. Instead the *do-er* who is not achieving their goals as fast as they would like uses the frustration generated to enquire and learn. But is it in *doing* that things get done.

In his book "Transformation", Robert A Johnson highlights the moment where Goethe's great character *Faust* makes a fundamental change.

> *Dissatisfied with the translation of the beginning line of the Gospel According to John, he [Faust] sets to work on a new translation. "In the beginning was the Word" is precisely the one-sided attitude that has bought such inertia to Faust, and it is this perspective that he now challenges. He strikes upon a new attitude for the beginning of his Gospel,*

"In the beginning was the Act," and a whole new
consciousness of life opens up to him.

It is in changing from the intellectualized thinking world of
"word" to the doing process of "act". I can learn all I want. I can
read every book, study with every guru, but eventually, I must
"DO". No amount of wining or complaining or procrastinating or
arguing or testing or theorizing or planning or promising will divert
us from this. To achieve anything we must "DO".

The basics of any business

We all have instinctive preferences that make the tasks we like
enjoyable, and the tasks we loathe eternally avoidable! But there
are a few fundamental elements that anyone setting up in business
must "DO" in order for that business to succeed – avoiding any of
these tasks massively increases the risk that we will fail in
business; conversely, diligently addressing these tasks, even if we
groan at the thought of doing them, can significantly help minimise
the risks of getting things wrong.

It is these more difficult tasks, the ones that do not come
intuitively to us, that we put off, procrastinate over and avoid. I
watched a television program recently about a lady who was
sinking her life savings into setting up her dream restaurant. She
had great enthusiasm for the project, a strong vision for what the
place should look like, the sort of food she wanted to serve and the
level of customer service she wanted to bring to her diners
experience. Yet she had done no market research (because she
was afraid of hearing that her idea sucked!), had not calculated
how much the ingredients were going to cost for her menu, or even
looked at the practicalities of running her restaurant like staffing
levels or costs.

At one point during the program, she was challenged by the
presenter (a chef who was experienced at setting up restaurants)
to sit down and cost her ingredients. She put this off at first, then

made excuses as to why it had not been done, and eventually broke down in tears when she was put on the spot about this task for a third time. This emotional reaction demonstrated precisely why we all procrastinate over those tasks we like the least – they evoke our anxieties. For her, it evoked a fear of numbers, fears over failure and of having her dream not live up to the vision that she'd had for many years.

She was risking her entire life savings on a hunch that she'd find the right staff willing to cook her recipes and work to her high standards, that the local (and somewhat conservative) population would embrace her choice in food, pay enough per meal to make it turn a moderate profit, and keep coming back time and again. Thankfully for her, having worked through some of these essential activities, she was able to turn her restaurant into a success.

The basics of any business, those questions that all business MUST ask in order to establish the viability of the business are these:

1. Do the people in my area want what I am proposing to offer?
2. Can I sell my product/service at a price that will enable me to turn a profit?
3. How much money do I need to invest in advance before I can become self-sufficient?
4. What practical barriers can I forecast that I will need to overcome?

Excuses, excuses ... and the delusion of security.

With no discipline, we overcome nothing. With some discipline, we overcome some things. With complete discipline, we overcome everything.

M Scott Peck, The Road Less Travelled

We are remarkable creatures. Over many thousands of years, we have adapted and survived, learning new skills and utilising an ever-developing intellect to grow in sophistication. We tamed the land and farmed crops. We built shelters to keep us warm. We created laws and the means for those laws to be policed.

Up until very recently in our evolution, human beings have been driven by Maslow's basics of life - warmth, food, security. These drivers pushed us to evolve out of necessity. Not learning how to build a shelter meant death of exposure. Not learning how to farm or trap animals meant starvation.

In our cosseted western society, the majority of these basic needs have been resolved. We have entered a consumer state where we are provided all manner of things to entertain us, but without the *necessity* to work hard to create warmth, food and security, it is now all too easy to not bother. This risks allowing ourselves to excuse ourselves from hard work, procrastinating and justifying why we shouldn't. We're always too busy, too tired, too stressed, or afraid of trying something new for fear of introducing unnecessary risk.

We delude ourselves with the idea that working as an employee gives us job security, and that we're safer staying where we are and not trying anything new.

Allow me to spell that statement out – just because we do not know the true financial position of a company we might be working for, or that we do not know the true intent of the shareholders/owners does not mean that we can pretend that our position is secure. This attitude is naive at best, and deluded at worst, something that anyone who has suddenly found themselves being made redundant knows only too well.

This negative risk-avoidant, stay-safe attitude kills our (natural) adventurous human spirit, kills our (natural) creativity, and stunts our ability to evolve ourselves beyond the limits of mere survival. I don't know about you, but I don't want to merely survive – I want to thrive!

Time is the fundamental constant. You can't buy more of it, and you can't get spent time back. Successful people maximise their time, turning it into productivity. They are not easily distracted from their focus. They do not idle their lives away watching endless television or fill their minds with useless tittle-tattle, or feed an anxiety with food. They watch sport to be inspired by the prowess of the athletes rather than endlessly wishing that they could be something they are not. When they make mistakes, they learn from them and try not to make that mistake again. They realise that success is built by achieving a single step every day, sometimes for many years, before their dreams come to fruition. They realise that to succeed, they have to use every precious second. They have to make sacrifices. They have to overcome setbacks rather than giving up at the first hurdle. They do not wait for the overwhelmingly unlikely event of a lotto win, to be given a million pounds - instead they determine to figure out how to sell a million things at a pound profit.

Be inspired by successful people. They are mere humans, just like you and me. And that means that you and me possess all we need to be as successful as them. If we want it bad enough to not allow our fear to stop us.

Workshop A – The rules of success

Use these rules as a 7-point plan to overcoming the barriers to success

1. Success comes through having a clear vision of what success looks like, through having clearly defined of goals - **set goals**

2. Success comes over time, through gradual, incremental steps towards stated goals - **set markers on the road**

3. Success come through hard work and determination in the face of fear and set backs - **understand what we do with failure, and how fear paralyses us**

4. Success comes through the self-discipline to do what needs to be done - **understand how we give up**

5. Success comes from not waiting for problems to be solved for us, but for us to solve them for ourselves, to learn new skills, to say "I don't know" rather than "I can't" - **develop a can-do attitude**

6. Success comes through allowing ourselves to think laterally as to how to solve a problem - **invite and consider other opinions**

7. Success comes from diligently doing the jobs we like the least – **Be professional and disciplined in doing the things we would rather avoid**

Consider also the basic questions that all business MUST ask in order to establish the viability of the business:

1. Do people in my area want what I am proposing to offer?
2. Can I sell my product/service at a price that will enable me to turn a profit?
3. How much money do I need to invest in advance before I can become self-sufficient?
4. What practical barriers can I foresee?

Section 2 – Essential marketing essentials

Marketing is not a black art. But like any profession, it develops a language all of its own that ends up being full of confusing terminology that few (even those in the profession) really understand. While marketing benefits from a creative flare, and from being able to write reasonably well (which is why the profession typically attracts creative people), the real skill is in being able to know and think like your consumers so that your marketing spend is geared towards bringing you clients.

In this section we will look at how buyer behaviour has developed over the past 50 years, and go on to develop a simple set of principles for you to follow when designing your own marketing strategy.

These principles will be illustrated by looking at common mistakes made by small business owners, mistakes that end up costing a lot of money with very little, if any, measurable return.

Finally, a workshop has been included that will help you develop a strategy that follows these principles so you can quickly and efficiently master what you need to know in order to succeed.

The demise of the General Store

There was a time, not so long ago, when the high street and the general store would cater for the majority of our needs. We could easily and quickly buy milk, bread, meat from the butcher, perhaps a tin of paint or a screwdriver from a hardware supplier, petrol and a newspaper. The school we attended was the one closest to us, and the industries and employers in our immediate locality governed the careers we went on to pursue.

These stores were part and parcel of the fabric of our society. Whilst we might look back on this time with a degree of nostalgia, the truth was that choice and availability of products for purchase was limited. A lack of local competition also meant that these stores could determine the price of products. With relatively little produce to choose from, we had to make do with what was available, and the General Store and the high street thrived and made reasonable profits from selling us every-day basics.

Things began to change significantly as more and more of us could afford to own a car. Now the general store was not our only choice, and out-of-town superstores sprang up and offered us three things – great prices, a breadth of choice never before dreamt possible, and the ability to browse at our leisure through produce at "self-service super markets".

General Stores quickly realised that they simply could not compete on price, freshness or product variety, and were forced to change. At first they tried to highlight their difference (to "differentiate" in marketing lingo) by emphasising their ability to offer personalised counter service and detailed product knowledge. Today they specialise by offering either convenience (for example opening late, and being close at hand for that extra pint of milk), or high-quality, high-priced produce (such as specialist delicatessens). And the effects of this are still very much in evidence today as once thriving high streets are becoming more and more derelict.

Our mobility was critical to this change – and it hasn't stopped with the relative ease of physical transportation. Today this mobility is driven by the Internet. Now the general store comes to us. In a matter of seconds, we can find *precisely* what we are looking for from suppliers anywhere in the world, and we can compare prices and place an order and let the product come to us.

This revolution has been further accelerated by the ubiquitous availability of Internet-ready mobile devices such as smart phones. Now the world comes to us wherever we are at any time of the day or night.

This is truly revolutionary, and the speed of this change has been quite incredible. For hundreds of years buyers have had to buy what was immediately available, from local producers and stores that were an integral part of local communities – in a matter of a few decades this has been radically replaced by vast choice and global competition.

Some mourn the loss of our high streets, and indeed most recently there has been something of a revival of popularity driven by stores selling "experience", fine produce delicatessens, coffee shops, specialist suppliers, coffee shops, hair-dressing salons, and more coffee shops! While the high street is still highly relevant for certain products (I prefer to try cloths on before I buy them, for instance), the high street has become a place to experience and browse where once it was a functional place, a place where we bought our groceries. But what will now never change is how buyers now behave.

Modern buyer behaviour

How is the Internet relevant to you? How can the Internet, with its global reach possibly be relevant to a private practitioner offering a local service? The answer is in how the Internet has revolutionised the way we find products and services.

The big change of the supermarket was choice and price. But the subtle change was in the way in which we could freely browse shelves and find new products. Instead of asking for what we wanted from behind the counter, we could now browse at our leisure, discover new products and make choice ourselves.

Shop owners liked it – it meant lower overheads in staff, which in turn meant improved profitability. Marketers liked it – it meant a more direct connection between advertising promotion and sales. And consumers liked it – now *they* were empowered to make choice.

With the Internet, the range of choices and the competitiveness of price have both improved, but perhaps only marginally. The big change with the Internet is in the anonymity and spontaneity of buyers, and crucially the way in which they search for products and services.

Originally, the Internet was merely a collection of linked computers. If you wanted to access the content on these computers, you needed to know the address. But to make matters worse, unlike memorable addresses like www.bbc.co.uk, the Internet was originally designated with a numerical code known as an IP Address such as 212.58.251.195. As the amount of content grew, it became necessary to use searching software to find specific content, and "Search Engines" were created. Today, Search Engines like Google[3] make it possible to search for almost anything in fractions of a second – and this has fundamentally changed modern buyer behaviour.

Think of it like this. An Internet site is like a shop front. Stores still have window displays, meant to capture our attention, identify what that store sells, and tempt the browsing buyer to wander in and look around. But where a high street or shopping centre might have 20-200 stores, the Internet has millions and millions of stores all on the same "high street". Search Engines are then like very helpful shop assistants who know every product of every store and present you with a range of alternatives that suit your needs, and then transport you to the exact location in the exact shop you need in a fraction of a second.

Even you, as a private practitioner, can have a "shop front" on the Internet. But unlike a store owner, you do not need to rent expensive shop space on a high street where you do not know how many people will walk past ("foot-fall" in Marketing speak).

Todays' buyers have become used to this level of specificity when searching. They use Search Engines to quickly finding exactly what they are looking for, and the searches they conduct are more and more phonetic, i.e. they search using the words that

---

[3] *We refer repeatedly to Google in this book. Google is not the only Search Engine, nor is it the only service offering advertising or analytical services. Google is, perhaps, the best known and possibly the most advanced company in the field, but we use Google as an inter-changeable term with the many and varied Internet Search Engine providers.*

they associate with their need rather than thinking too hard about the "correct" term - they use the power of Search Engines to do the boring browsing for them, narrowing searches to home in on the specific products they seek.

So, rather than searching for a specific product, by product name, they search for their need, for a resulting satisfaction or pain relief or psychological difficulty. Lets illustrate this with a few examples:

- Buyers do not search for specific services such as "Podiatrist" unless they are already educated to know what they need – instead they search for "ingrowing toenail" or "toe pain" or "it hurts to wear high-heels". The Search Engine then displays content, and the buyer quickly learns that a Podiatrist is needed. Then they might go further and search for "toe pain help Birmingham", and the Search Engine will return even more specific information about services in that area.

- Another example might be a search conducted for "back pain" rather than for "Physiotherapist". The Search Engine displays content, and the buyer quickly learns that a physiotherapist can help cure persistent back pain. Then they might go further and search for "back pain cure Edinburgh", and the Search Engine will return even more specific information about services in that area.

- Additionally, buyers do not search for named individuals or businesses unless they already know them. So they will not search for "Mrs Miggin's Pie Shop" unless they specifically know to look for Mrs Miggin's, perhaps by recommendation or some other (expensive) advertising campaign. Instead they might search for "home made pies". The Search Engine then displays content, and the buyer quickly learns that there is a shop run by Mrs Miggin's that sells home made pies.

All of this is relevant because in a similar way, potential counselling clients typically do not search for "Therapist" or "John

Kennett Counselling" – but they do search for "anger help" or "relationship advice Manchester" or "my daughter is cutting herself" or "am I a sex addict?"

This leads us to our first principal for small business marketing – you must **think like your customer** and arrange your product offering to **answer the questions your customers are likely to ask**. By aligning the content and structure of your website to answer the need of your potential clients, you are far more likely to be found in amongst the many service providers.

A useful way of understanding this is to think in terms of pain. When we cut ourselves, our body sends a message to our brain that we interpret as pain. This response triggers us to instinctively reach for the injury, releasing hormones that are designed to help us react and heal. If we apply that to our potential clients, we can see that the pain – in this case the psychological pain – is the driving force for action, and it is this that will, eventually, lead them to view your website and pick up the phone.

So the Podiatrist in the above example should not promote "all your podiatry needs taken care of" because it means nothing to the uneducated potential customer and will not be how the customer will conduct their search. Instead, they should promote "quick and effective solutions for ingrowing toenails". That way, when the customer begins to search *in the way that they are likely to search*, they quickly find a service that can help them solve a problem.

Similarly, the Physiotherapist should not seek to emphasise that they are "professionally trained with CSP membership" because it means nothing to anyone outside the profession, or the uneducated potential customer. Instead, they should align their service to the way in which the customer is likely to search and offer "professional advice and treatment for persistent back pain".

As for Mrs Miggin's, her pies might be well contain "the best locally sourced, organic ingredients", but that is not necessarily what the customer is going to be searching for – instead, it is more likely that the customer will respond better to an offer of "a home made, tasty alternative for your lunch".

Principal 1 – Align your service offering to address the pain your customers are facing

Another important factor to keep in mind is just how lazy this powerful search tool has made people. There is a substantial amount of evidence that when people search Google, they expect to find what they are looking for very quickly. Google will often produce thousands of references to a search, but people rarely search anything more than the first page, or even scroll down from the first half of the first page. For this reason, it is important that your page appears as high as possible on the first page of search results (Google call this "ranking"), a topic we will cover in more detail under "Making your website work for you" later in this section.

Highly specific = highly desirable

The second principal centres around the way customers respond to offers that are specific to their needs.

Imagine that the exhaust on your Nissan Micra suddenly falls off. It's raining, you're running late for work and you have previously had bad experienced with garages selling you more than you needed because of your lack of mechanical know-how. Not a great way to start the day.

As you nurse the car to the side of the road, you look up and to your delight you realise that you've pulled over right outside a garage. Above the door a sign reads "The Nissan Micra Exhaust Centre". What good luck! A notice on the front door reads, "Exhausts fitted while-you-wait, no appointment needed. 25% off for new customers, and a loyalty scheme for our valued repeat customers." In disbelief, you peer through the glass and you see a welcoming waiting-room with comfortable looking seating and a smartly dressed receptionist who notices you and comes to the door with an umbrella and a warm smile.

Good luck indeed. But this is precisely what the Internet and Search Engines are able to offer. Just when you need something specific, a Search Engine will help you find precisely what you're looking for, even for really complex requests.

This is a useful moment to illustrate the biggest single mistake made by service providers – they are difficult to differentiate from their competitors. Let's go back to the broken exhaust again. Had you pulled over and seen nothing more than an anonymous industrial unit, you would not have known that tantalisingly close, just behind that roller door, was an exhaust centre. All you would have seen was an anonymous industrial unit. Even if it had a sign – "Bob's car repairs" – you might have tried the door, but you could not possibly guess that it was a specialist exhaust centre. Now you look beyond the immediate location you have pulled up and see one industrial unit after another, all similarly bland looking garages. Had there been a sign for a specialist exhaust centre half a mile in the distance, you'd have pushed the damn car to that garage just because it was specific about what it offered.

Mistake 1 – Focusing too much on you, rather than focusing on the problem

Let's translate that to counselling websites. The vast majority of private practitioners make this classic mistake – "John Kennett Counselling", my qualifications, my background and "What is counselling" means nothing to the potential customer conducting his/her search, especially when there are a dozen other sites all offering exactly the same. The potential customer is not searching for "John Kennett" or "Jason Colyer". They want help!

Similarly, they don't know and don't care about the modality you operate. "The London Humanistic Counselling Centre" means as much to the average person as "The London Bingy-Bangy Counselling Centre". At best, it might be fashionable because a particular technique was featured in Cosmopolitan magazine, but it still struggles to make a good connection between the pain the individual is experiencing and the service they require.

This leads us to Principal 2 – *occupy a niche*, and attract customers that are looking for a specific service. This means focusing your service on offering help for specific problems, helping individuals to be signposted to your door. Later on in this section is Workshop B – finding your niche where we will guide you through the process.

Principal 2 – Occupy a niche: Design your service to reach a very specific niche, and have as many niche 'shop fronts' as you like!

This is counter-intuitive because it goes against our experience with the General Store, and even the Super-Market. For these older buyer behaviour models, the way to succeed was to offer as wide a range of products as possible and stack-them-high-sell-them-cheap. This made logical sense for the retailer seeking to maximise the geographical foot-fall potential of his/her expensive retail unit. But the post-geographically specific Internet is fundamentally different – different in the way that customers find you, and therefore customers respond in a completely different way when compared to the old models.

It is reasonable to presume that by being a niche provider you limit your customer base, but offering a niche product has numerous advantages:

- The customer is far more likely to find your service in amongst the millions of others because by being highly specific in what you offer, you stand out from the crowd. In Internet Search Engine terms, this is known as "relevance" and helps propel your website to the top of the search results.
- Similarly, having a highly specific offering means that you will have less direct competition. This does not

mean that there are fewer counsellors out there able to offer excellent help with the specific problems you are niching to, but it does mean that the potential customer is *far* more likely to find – and choose – you.

- Because you are offering a specific service, the customer is more likely to trust that your service is able to answer their specific needs, and this helps encourage them to pick up the 'phone and make that booking. See <u>delivering Confidence (part of "A.I.D.C.A.")</u> below.
- Finally, because of the way that Internet advertising works, a niche product has less services competing for that advertising space, helping to keep your advertising costs down and your click-through-to-conversion-rate high. More on that later.

While being a niche player undoubtedly slices your total potential audience down, because you do not have the overheads of an expensive shop front, you can have as many "shop fronts" – i.e. web sites – as you want. Imagine a car garage that could afford to have shop fronts offering a "specialist exhaust centre" for every make and model of car in the country. Prohibitively expensive in real terms, but achievable for the Internet. The inexpensive nature of a website means that there is little stopping you from having 5 or 5000 websites, all offering a specific niche service, but all actually being serviced by you.

A.I.D.C.A. – attracting and closing leads

Once you have decided on your niche, it will be time to think about creating marketing materials – especially a website – for you to attract potential customers. This is a critical moment as a common mistake is to create marketing materials without having a clear niche identified. The result of this mistake is a hotchpotch of material that does not communicate anything tangible. The poor results gained from this material leave it being a real waste of money.

Mistake 2 – Wasting money on promotion without a clear niche

The niche *must* define your brand because of the final piece of the Buyer Behaviour jigsaw, a purchasing "pathway" summarised through an acronym known as A.I.D.C.A., which stands for Attention, Interest, Desire, Confidence and Action.

This purchasing pathway is followed unconsciously by all of us all of the time when we buy anything. It starts with us experiencing a driving impulse, an emotion, a need or a want. When we are in this frame of mind, marketing messages are more likely to grab our attention, causing us to notice something to which we would not otherwise have paid much attention. You can test this for yourself – the advertising you are most likely to recall is advertising that is relevant to you in some way, and it caused you to store it away.

Professional marketers use a wide range of methods of getting your Attention, grab your Interest, and to generate Desire. They influence the media (and increasingly the social media) to favourably portray a brand, through targeted marketing and through advertising, and by creating demand by suggesting problems.

Marketers are responsible for subtly suggesting that a car will enhance your image, that a face cream (which is, of course, "scientifically proven") will reduce wrinkles, or that you can avoid the dangers of dehydration by drinking specially filtered bottled water. The truth is that I do not need a car to enhance my image – I merely need to get from A to B; I was not previously concerned about facial wrinkles (and, honestly, I am still not concerned!); and if my cat can manage to maintain a high level of hydration without carrying a bottle of mineral water, then I'm sure I can too!

But the reason it works is because marketers have been sure to carefully define the demographic profile of the target customer before creating any marketing materials. This is why car sales are predominantly targeted a male audience, face cream at middle-aged women, and mineral water at individuals interested in sport – each audience has been identified as being susceptible to being concerned about image/wrinkles/hydration respectively.

Marketers will then spend a considerable amount of time and effort defining a brands' "identity", describing it with words and images and emotions. By doing this, they are able to ensure that the marketing communications is consistent with the target market, increasing its effectiveness. Thankfully, we do not need to be so detailed, but the methods remain the same.

Attention, Interest and Desire are important concepts to grasp, not for Counselling *per say*, but for your niche. Many individuals will know about counselling, but they might not know of the relevance to them. This is why a niche service for bereavement or post-natal depression might grab Attention, and by suggesting how your service might help individuals overcome their emotional pain would create Interest and Desire.

This leads us to our third principal, making sure that what you say in your marketing materials (crucially, your website) is a result of who you are aiming your materials at, and the emotional drivers they are likely to be experiencing.

Principal 3 – Ensure your identified niche defines your brand, not the other way around

This raises an ethical dilemma. Marketers, driven by shareholder need to create market demand for a product or service, have used these techniques to create demand where demand never previously existed. Indeed, the man considered the "Father of Public Relations"[4], Eddie Bernays, has been attributed as the man responsible for creating demand amongst women to smoke cigarettes in the early 20th Century by paying leading female movie stars to smoke at a time when women were looking for ways to assert themselves in a male dominated world. Eddie Bernays made acceptable something that was previously socially unacceptable, made it fashionable, and coined the phrase "torches of freedom" that women could hold up with pride.   He also happened to be the nephew of Sigmund Freud, and spent his summers with Freud in Austria discussing the psychology of the mind.

While talk of Attention, Interest and Desire might be seen as flirting with the important ethical stance of The **Business of Counselling**, it is worth recalling here how it is that people search for counselling services. If you recall our first principal – that of aligning your service to address the pain your customers face – we remember that customers are actively searching for solutions to their problems. So, ironically, thinking in terms of Attention, Interest and Desire could equally be seen as helping people access counselling services by helping them understand that counselling is relevant to their need. I regularly meet new clients who say "I read the list of symptoms on your website and ticked every one!" They also tell me that they typically would never have considered counselling as being something they would try in order to resolve their issues. The simple way to avoid problems is to try and avoid making unfounded promises, either overtly in text statements, or implied through images.

---

[4] *The Father of Spin: Edward L. Bernays & the birth of public relations (2002), by Larry Tye*

Confidence

The next part of this Purchasing Pathway is Confidence. We tend to buy from brands we trust, staying loyal with these brands for many years even if the next product on the shelf is half the price and ostensibly the same. When we buy a new car, confidence is critical to the manufacturer or model we choose, as is our experience of the individual sales person who is selling us that car. And even though a house purchase is probably the single largest expenditure item most of us will experience, we still tend to use our hearts rather than our heads to inform us about that purchase based on our opinion of the people who lived there before, what the neighbours are like or whether or not the estate agent is someone we believe has our best interest at heart.

Confidence is _the_ key stumbling block for prospective clients looking for a counsellor because they are about to entrust their emotions to us at their moment of greatest vulnerability. Prospective clients browsing through the many and various web pages have already paid Attention, taken an Interest and developed a Desire – what they are waiting for is Confidence, Confidence that you will be able to help them, "contain" them, tolerate them, not judge them, and not betray them.

Mentioning the length and breadth of your experience, your qualifications and professional affiliations is a basic minimum in establishing Confidence. Make sure that the content of your website also includes text that demonstrates your understanding, for example by including "common symptoms" or case study type material that pertains to your identified niche.

Think also about the images you include. So many counsellor websites seem to include pseudo-spiritual images of snacked pebbles or flowers. Images such as these mean nothing and something. Perhaps they are telling your prospective audience that you're a Buddhist?! Such images are probably only relevant if your identified niche is based on working in a modality that uses meditation or Eastern philosophy? But do they instil Confidence?

Probably not. Actually, one might argue that such images are off-putting to many prospective clients.

I conducted an interesting experiment with my website where I ran one version for three months where I referred to myself by name only (exposing my gender, but not my age, ethnicity etc.) and then three months by including a photograph of myself. The difference was stark – the site with a photograph got considerably more interest. New clients would state how they felt reassured that the person they would be meeting appeared to be "accessible" or "normal". Even the photo I chose was deliberately one of me in a T-shirt showing a little of the tattoo on my right arm, rather than one of me in a suit. **It won't appeal to everyone, but it will appeal to the majority of my target niche for this web site** – and that's the point. If I want to reach a different audience then I will need another website that promotes my services to that specific audience, and maybe my tattoo is not to be shown in that instance.

Confidence can be further enhanced by including interesting articles, or even a blog page. But if you're going to do this, don't loose sight of why you're doing this – to instil confidence in the mind of the prospective client in your identified niche that you understand their needs, not to impose an attitude or opinion on potential clients in advance. Anything you write and publish in this way needs to underline your specialism, encouraging the reader to identify with you and your message.

Ask yourself how you think you are going to be perceived. Ask for, and listen to, the feedback you get from your clients about your site (we'll look more at this in the Practice Management Systems section of this book). Think about what impression you're creating. Would you buy a car from a bloke you've never met who has given you a mobile phone number, wants to meet you at an unknown location, and only wants to do a transaction in cash? Probably not. We want a land-line number, an address, a reputation, a responsible individual in whom we can trust. Counselling clients want to feel the same level of confidence, and our job is to do all we can to create that confidence.

Principal 4 – Create confidence in your service

<u>*Action*</u>

Finally in our Purchasing Pathway is Action. All good advertising will prompt us to find out more, go to a website, follow via a social media mechanism like Facebook or Twitter, or some incentivised purchasing offer. Your marketing material, especially your website, needs to do the same. It should be easy for your prospective clients to contact you via a method that *they* prefer. And it should be really obvious – i.e. prominent – on your materials.

As a minimum, you should include an email address and a mobile phone number (for calls and for SMS/text messaged), and ideally a "land-line" phone number as well to help instil that all important confidence. And if on your website you can include an email form within your site (i.e. a message is sent to you from within your website rather than requiring them to open their email application and copy your email address) – you make it easier still for people to contact you.

Principal 5 – Always include a "call to action", and make it easy for customers to contact you

The Marketing Mix

No matter how good your service is, it is unlikely that clients will beat a path to your door without some form of marketing activity. But how should you advertise your service to the world? How much money is reasonable to spend on what sort of marketing, and what returns are you likely to get from different promotional methods?

Almost as soon as you "go public" with your service, you're likely to start getting phone calls from marketing companies trying to persuade you to part with your hard earned cash for advertising in this magazine or that website, or for web design, or for "Search Engine Optimisation". Navigating your way through this requires a basic understanding of the Marketing Mix, and two simple rules to apply (see Principals 8 & 9 below) that will help keep your return on marketing investment high.

The "Marketing Mix" is made up of what's known as "The 4 P's" – Product, Price, Place, & Promotion. We will focus our attention mostly on the last of these, but it is worth you knowing the basics of the first three.

Product

We have already covered at length the merits of a niche product focused on a niche audience. Your "product" is this specialist niche service, much more than merely a "counselling service", rather a "counselling service designed to help a specific group or audience".

Having a clear definition of your "Product" is really useful as it helps your marketing effort by reminding you, and therefore focusing you on what your product is and is not, so that you can better navigate your way through what is good marketing and what is not worth the investment.

When you have completed Workshop B, you should have a clear description of your product, defined in terms of what it is, who is it aimed at (gender, age, ethnicity, presenting problem), and how it is meant to help that group. Knowing this sort of detail helps create a reference point for your product when thinking about promotional activities, batting away irrelevant or dubious offers, and helping you hone in on those that may be of some benefit.

Price

Here, marketers seek to understand how much can justifiably be charged for a service. They set price based on "price tolerance", i.e. how much a chosen customer group is willing to pay for a product or service, studying both competition and "value" – the treatment that cures debilitating back pain has a very high "value" if you're suffering, whereas a new shampoo can only command a ceiling price no matter how good it is because there are a wide range of alternative products.

Many make the mistake of determining price based on what they need to afford to charge, merely calculating the cost and adding a margin determined by how much they would like to earn. We must, of course, take into account the cost of providing the service – after all, no business enterprise will ever work if there isn't enough income from providing that service to cover costs – but it may be wildly different from what people in your group are willing to pay.

Principal 6 - Price needs to be ethically set on what your accessible market is willing to pay

Let's break this statement down.

- Your market = the niche group you have identified described in terms of the value you bring to those individuals
- Accessible = the geographical reach your product has based on how willing your clients are to travel to receive your service
- Willing to pay = the perception of value your product brings

Like all equations, it is a balancing act.

Perceived value + greater specialism = willingness of specific potential customers to travel and pay for your service.

So, if a physiotherapist can demonstrate that s/he can perform a specialist technique that works for 90% of chronic back pain sufferers, that practitioner will be able to charge more and the clients will show a greater willingness to travel to receive that specialist service. Conversely, if a generic counselling practice is offered in London where there are many practitioners and travel is easy, then the price you are able to charge will be relatively low.

This underlines why a specialist approach is critical to the success of a private practice. For counsellors, this is can be a thorny issue, especially if you are relatively inexperienced or if you are seeking to provide a service to a group that is likely to struggle to pay (although this latter group can be helped by attempting to secure some funding to cover or subsidise the cost of providing the service).

The simple route to determining how much you should charge will be based on doing some basic research in your area (geographic area and specialism area) and looking at what others are charging. If you're starting out, you'll be looking to get your income going as quickly as possible, so charging less than average makes sense. Research 10 other providers (look at their websites) and take an average, then go under that price by 10% or 20% to get going.

Keep in mind that established, experienced private practitioners are likely to charge more for their service simply because they have reached a comfortable volume of regular clients and have higher fees because they do not need to be attracting larger volumes of clients to fill their diaries. The practitioners that are keen to promote their services (through advertising etc.) are likely to have established a more competitive price for their service, and it is this that should be your initial steer as to what to charge.

Another thing to keep in mind is how your clients are likely to pay. If the average works out at £47.63, and you undercharge by 10% (£4.76), then mathematically, you're looking at £47.63 - £4.76 = £42.87. It is sensible to round this to the nearest £5 – say £40 or £45, helping to keep things simple with client transactions.

Once you've determined your price, you need to check that it's going to be worthwhile based on costs. (Note that we're doing this *after* we've established price tolerance!) Add up all your likely expenditure for a month. Here is a quick table of typical expenses:

Room rent (per month)	£250
Supervision (per month)	£120
Insurance (per month)	£15
BACP/BPS membership (per month)	£15
Telephone (per month)	£25
Marketing costs (per month)	£100
Total (per month)	£525

In order to make £1000 per month in "earnings" (profit) to you, you're going to need to take £1525 per month in fees. At £40 per client, that's about 38 clients a month, or approximately 9 clients a week.

You will note that this principal refers to a price being "ethically" set. Making a "reasonable" profit is important. Profiteering from people's pain is unethical – making a living is not. Does a therapist on Harley Street charging £150 a session wearing an Armani suit really offer better therapy than the practitioner two streets down who charges £35 a session? Probably not. But if the Harley Street therapist is highly specialised, and has a reputation for working with the utmost discretion for high-profile individuals, then maybe £150 a session is reasonable.

A further ethical consideration is about remaining "fit to practice". The BACP suggest that 24 clients per week would be a workable maximum, and our experience is that this is about right. But keep in mind that your numbers will rise and fall according to how successful your marketing efforts are, whether there are school holidays, whether your clients want to see you weekly, fortnightly etc., and your own capacity, both in terms of time and emotional capacity.

Place

For the marketer, *Place* encompasses a range of geographical and physical considerations, separated into three groups.

The first group of considerations is designed to ask you to question where in the country you establish your service. This is important as you need to be realistic about whether or not you can reach a sufficiently large accessible market of target clients (based on your niche) to make your practice viable.

The second group of considerations asks how easy it is for your potential clients to get to you? How easy is it for them to park or walk from public transport hubs? And importantly for counselling services, does the location of the service help to maintain the clients' feeling of anonymity?

The third group of considerations is based around the appearance of your practice room. Ideally, this should reflect the brand identity that you have established for your practice. For example, would a service aimed at substance misuse work in your front room, or would a service aimed at teenagers work in a room that is completely un-cool?!

Principal 7 – The setting of you practice should reflect your niche and be conveniently accessible for a large enough market

Town centres are excellent places to begin your search. Many town centres will have empty office units and community centres, with plenty of parking options and ease of access. They also help clients maintain anonymity by giving them a viable excuse to be in town.

If you plan to set up a practice at home, there are a number of factors to consider. How easy is it to park? How will other members of your household be in dealing with the need for discretion, peace and quiet? How private is this space for your clients? Is an upstairs converted bedroom space *too* intimate? How feasible is it to create a space that is not too imprinted with your personality? What might your neighbours say/think? What will your clients feel turning up at someone's house at all times of the day? What safety considerations are required – remember, your clients will know where you live! And don't forget that you will need liability insurance to cover any mishaps on your property. Financially, it is tempting to set up at home, but this needs to be tested against your target niche, and balanced with your need to have a private life.

In recent years, there has been an increase in the prevalence of on-line based services, either VoIP (Voice over Internet Protocol) or web-cam video communication such as Apples' FaceTime. While these have the potential to work, it is important to consider how these are perceived by your potential client group – does an online service help give access to a group that would otherwise not be able to gain access to your service? Or is it merely a way for you to practice from your villa in Tuscany?!

Promotion

When most of us think about Marketing, most of us identify with the many promotional activities that marketers undertake to get market share. But how should you promote your service? What techniques work and what do not? How much money should you spend on different marketing activities? There are many different promotional techniques available to marketers to reach any given target audience from TV advertising to in-store promotions, and from list rental mail-shots to browsing history based internet advertising, but for our purposes we need to break them into three broad groups – "push", "discovery" and "educational".

"Push" techniques are those that "push" the promotional message at potential customers. They include print (newspaper or magazine) advertising, billboards and A-frames, flyers, exhibitions and public fares, emailers and postal mailings. They are characterised by the way in which the promotion is overt or in-your-face. Here marketers compete with the many other advertisers that are seeking to win a slice of your mind share, and so tend to be expensive.

They also tend to not be specific enough to accurately target specific groups, at best attracting broad if disparate groups of individuals based on reader profiles. They rely on that Goldilocks moment – not too hot, not too cold – to be in the right place, at the right time, with the right message to attract your attention and grab your interest at a moment where a buyer might take up an offer. Having gone to all the trouble of defining a niche, and with the high associated costs, these techniques tend to be very wasteful for the private practitioner. They are also dubious in ethical terms as they tend to focus on a specific problem (depression, anger, etc.), and tend to offer an all-but-guaranteed solution to what is probably a complex problem. Think of those dating agency adverts – they all typically include a happy, smiley couple at the end of the advert, the implication being that you too can find love.

More useful to private practitioners are the "discovery" promotional techniques. As we have previously outlined in **Modern Buyer Behaviour** above, our clients are far more likely to search for specific information based on their specific needs at a specific moment. With "discovery" promotional techniques, it is a Goldilocks moment every time a search is conducted. The job of this marketing technique is to be as easy to be found as possible, and then "convert" the browsing potential customer to take Action and make an appointment.

"Educational" techniques are about providing information, which subtly builds confidence in the readers mind. Techniques include brochures, flyers and websites, on-line blog pages, interviews and articles published in print or online newspapers or magazines. Another educational technique gaining in popularity is social media, providing a rich blend of "discovery" and "education".

Before we go into more detail and look at how you can use the various promotional techniques, we want to introduce you to the first of two simple principals that will help you focus and hone your promotional strategy.

Determining your promotion strategy

The phone rings. Could this be a new client enquiry? With anticipation in my voice I answer in the best phone manner I know.

"Hello, John Kennett speaking – how can I help you?"

"Hello John – my name is Arthur. Are you interested in growing your business?" My heart sinks. This is a classic opening patter from annoying, paid-on-commission sales juniors (they give themselves grandiose titles like "business development executives"). I'd love to say "no" and hang up the phone, but I can't quite bring myself to do so, nor can I find a witty retort to such a closed question.

"Yes – I guess", I reply hesitantly.

"Great," Arthur replies, thinking he's got me where he wants me. "I work for a local magazine that reaches 100,000 people in your area, and I have had a cancellation on a page of advertising that normally costs £1500 but my sales manager has let me sell it for half that price – £750 – and I wondered if you'd be interested in taking this opportunity to reach 100,000 potential new customers?"

Smugly, Arthur leaves the question (to which I have only just answered "yes") hanging in the air. What Arthur doesn't realise it that I've been in the marketing game since before he was an itch is his father's pants. This should be fun.

"Sounds interesting Arthur – 100,000 people you say? Wow, that's a lot. Can you tell me about the type of person the magazine is aimed at?" I ask, already beginning to tee him up for a kill shot.

"Err, yep. The reader profile is made up of men and women in Kent, typically with families," replies Arthur confidently.

Arthur's answer does not fill me with confidence. Magazines worth their salt do very detailed reader profiling. Indeed, many have to have their readership details independently audited so that they can show advertisers with some certainty what the profile of the readership is – age groups, gender distribution, employment status, even a classification of disposable income levels. I suspect that Arthur's magazine is little more than a home-grown, hand distributed type of magazine with a print run of about 25,000 and a presumed pass-on readership of 4 people per copy, 4 x 25,000 = 100,000.

"How long has the magazine been going Arthur?"

"We're on our 3rd issue now, and going from strength to strength," he replies with more than a heavy hint of arrogance in his voice. But 3 issues confirms what I need to know – this is not an audited magazine. Time to have some fun.

"Just so that I can clarify, because I'm sure you've done your research [snigger], but who do you think *my* customers are, Arthur?"

"Well, I presume that your clients are men?"

Well, stone me – this guy is good. With a company name like *Kent Counselling for Men*, Arthur is clearly a considerable intellect. I keep digging.

"That's right Arthur – so how many *men* read your magazine?"

"Err, about 50% of the readership, I think," he replied uncertainly.

"You think – can you show me the auditors report to confirm that?"

"We are still waiting for the auditors report to be finalised. As I said, we're only on our 3rd issue, and ..."

I cut him off. "So Arthur, if you're not audited, how can you be sure of the 100,000 readership? And how can you be sure that your magazine is read by the people I am interested in reaching?"

"Well it's an estimate based on our own research," he said digging himself ever deeper.

"An estimate?!" I lay the incredulity on extra thick.

"Yes, our research shows that the magazine is distributed to 20,000 house holds and is read by an average of 5 people per house hold."

I felt sorry for Arthur. Making sales calls like this is a thankless task requiring elephant-thick skin and the capacity to pick up the phone to the next person on the list and do it all again with unwavering enthusiasm. Lesser men would have just hung up, but to Arthur's credit, he stuck with it.

"So, let me get this clear Arthur – you print 20,000 copies, distribute them via some vague method, and you presume that they are read by an average of 5 people per household, some of whom might just be men? OK, tell me about the editorial bias – is it focused on men's issues? Men's interests? Who writes your editorial content?"

"The editor writes a review of the issue with additional editorial contributed by some of the advertisers – perhaps you would like to write an editorial? I can probably swing this with my sales manager?" It was Arthur's last stand.

"Arthur," I said bluntly, "how does all this sound to you? If you were in my position, what would you do? Of course I am keen to grow my business, and I'm not afraid of spending money on well targeted marketing, but you're not filling me with any degree of confidence that your publication has anything much to do with my target customers, and you want £750 for that? How many leads do you think I would receive? If I spent £750 on Internet advertising, I know – because I've got the evidence myself – that I would get about 1 new client for every £20 I spend, so that's about 35 new clients. Sorry Arthur, it's a no from me!"

This example demonstrates how we believe you should approach any promotional marketing activity for your private practice – ruthlessly questioning the relevance and anticipated effectiveness of any proposed activity, and only go for those activities where the return on investment is likely to be worth it.

Principal 8 – Ruthlessly question the relevance of any marketing activity, and only invest in those that give the best results

So in the example above, I questioned Arthur about the circulation and the relevance of the publication to my target audience to get an idea of what volume of leads I might expect, and it came up short. If I could design a really great advert, I might achieve a moderate amount of bookings from those few relevant readers, but the cost was fixed at £750 and there was no proof that my target audience would be get to see the advert anyway. Had the magazine been a "men's issues" publication, with a demonstrable circulation, it might have been a more attractive proposition. By contrast, knowing that advertising on the Internet can, on average, net me a new client for every £20 I spend is compelling data, especially when each new client stays for an average of 12 sessions.

Let's take this principal and look at the most common promotional activities undertaken by marketers. We will cover the benefits and pitfalls of each as we head towards a suggested strategy for your business.

Print advertising

As we have already seen in the example of Arthur, print advertising (that's any advertising in material that is printed on paper and published) is difficult to show strong return-on-investment. It is better suited to large brands that seek to increase sales of product and increase the awareness of the brand in the mind of potential buyers.

Factors critical to success of print advertising for the private practitioner include clear relevance of the readership to the target audience of the practice, good advertising design, and a willingness – and budget – to commit to advertising with a publication for a period of time in order to build an awareness among the audience.

This is why advertising-space-has-suddenly-become-available offers, like the one offered to me by Arthur, should immediately arouse your suspicion. Far better to go on the search for relevant publications yourself, asking clients what they read and doing some research into what publications might show promise.

But the costs involved make print advertising difficult to justify for the private practitioner, especially when there are more attractive options for your precious marketing spend.

Printed directories

One alternative to printed adverts might be in printed directories like Yellow Pages or Thompson Local. These were once the place to look for local services, but have fallen out of favour in the Internet age. Typically, directory publishers now include on-line replication of your printed advert as part of an overall package.

They tend to be expensive when compared with targeted on-line advertising, and you can only really be listed under "counselling", limiting your ability to focus your listing on your identified niche. However, depending upon your audience, it may still be worth investing in these directories.

Flyers and special promotions

We are all familiar with promotional offers. Buy one get one free, introductory discounts, loyalty schemes and competitions are familiar to us all, especially in the supermarket.

My enterprising local gym regularly runs promotions to recruit new members, with sporty looking staff standing in the high-street handing out printed flyers to passers by. And any one week will see my letter box stuffed with printed promotional flyers offering pizza delivery, Indian take away and kebabs of any flavour.

They work because of the relatively low cost of print and distribution – you can buy 10,000 for a matter of a few hundred pounds – and because the offer is enticing (providing you like pizza, Indian food and Kebabs, of course!)

The question for the private practitioner is, once again, about the relevance of the promotion to your audience. I have successfully run half-price introductory sessions for my new clients as an enticement to make that all important step into the practice room and get their first taste of counselling, and their first experience of me, before committing to a series of sessions at full price, but this offer is available to those individuals who come searching for my service via my website – it is not thrust in the hand of a random stranger on a flyer emblazoned with "half price introductory offer" in bold lettering!

In a profession seeking to empower autonomy and respect confidentiality, discretion is the name of the game. Flyers are, therefore, inappropriate, and promotions run with thoughtful consideration.

Business cards and brochures

Business cards and printed brochures make more sense for the private practitioner. A good quality business card helps to make a professional impression, can easily be concealed by the self-conscious client, be passed on to a friend, or be used to write the time and date of the next appointment on the reverse side of the card.

Brochures are also worth having available, especially if you are able to get them displayed in local information racks like those sometimes seen in doctors surgeries.

The relatively low cost of cards and brochure printing mean that these items are valuable to the private practitioner. And by ensuring that your business cards, brochures and websites all share the same design thoughts (colours, images, fonts), the professional look is further enhanced.

Email marketing & list rental

Email marketing has become a major battlefield in marketing. The huge benefit of email marketing is the almost zero-cost of delivering millions of emails to people anywhere in the world. However, as the number of people with an email address grew, so did the prevalence of SPAM email and email borne computer viruses.

The original idea was that marketers would build company databases to collect the email details of individuals who were either customers or potential customers. Then, they would periodically send them news and special offers to keep them interested in the product. While this remains a great way of staying in touch with interested contacts, abuse of data has meant an increase in SPAM to the point where laws had to be introduced.

The Data Protection Act 1998 gives the courts power to prosecute those who fail to securely store and responsibly use personal contact details, including electronic details such as email.

Good practice now involves building email lists based on an active "opt-in" action from the individual. This is why, when you, say, book a flight online and give your email address, you are invited to tick a box to give your permission for that company to stay in touch with you for things other than that specific flight. The risk to companies for not complying with this is that they might be "black-listed" by the Internet Service Providers (ISP's) and be blocked by individuals and/or companies, as well as leaving themselves open to the threat of prosecution under the Data Protection Act.

It is feasible that private practitioners might look at email as a way of staying in touch with clients, perhaps sending snippets of wisdom or book reviews. If someone actively opts-in to this form of communication, and they are given a simple and secure opt-out mechanism, and the data is absolutely secure, then maybe it might be useful. However, the risks of getting this wrong are substantial versus the potential gains from a marketing point of view. And my psycho-dynamic supervisor would have a field day exploring what this would mean for me and for my clients.

You may be approached by companies offering email list rentals. Magazines who have invested a great deal of time and effort in building and maintaining an audited circulation list of their publications sometimes seek to get more return on their list investment by selling access to the list to other companies. You may well have seen phrases like "we will share your details with specially selected partners" when signing up to an email newsletter etc. When you do this, you give that company permission to sell your data to other companies, the "specially selected" element being the simple fact that if you've bought, say, a flight, you're probably going to be interested in hotels or travel insurance. Similarly, if that data includes personal information such as age, gender, an address etc., then your data could be sold to a company seeking to reach, say, men aged 30-40 in London.

If you get a call offering you a list purchase, you should treat it the same way we treated Arthur at the beginning of this section. Scrutinise who the audience is and how clean the data is.

That said, ask yourself how you would feel getting an email from someone you've never heard of offering you counselling services. We would suggest that this is simply not an appropriate way of marketing counselling services.

Websites

As we have already outlined, a website for your private practice presents a wonderful opportunity to market successfully for relatively little cost. Once up and running, they remain ever-available for those who come looking for your service. Prospects can read about you and your service in private at a time that suits them, understand a little of what to expect, and then send you an email to make a booking. All while you sleep!

These factors make websites *the* marketing tool for private practitioners. Later on, (in "Making your website work for you") we will cover the mechanics of building your own website step-by-step, and look at how to increase the likelihood of your site being found among the millions of sites available.

Online advertising

If you have ever searched for anything on Google, you will have seen examples of online advertising. These are the "sponsored links" that appear on the top and right hand side of the Google search screen, and they have been set up and paid for individuals who are seeking to attract customers for specific products.

Unlike print media advertising, online advertising has many benefits similar to those already highlighted with having your own website. Such advertising is:

- Highly specific, driven by what is entered into a search engine by the person searching. This is achieved by selecting key words or phrases and associating them with your advert so that when someone searches for "Anger management, London", your anger counselling advert appears and is linked to a specific anger counselling page on your website.
- Charged for as it is used rather than merely buying space on a page and hoping that it yields a return. With online advertising, you pay for each click on your advert ("pay per click"), so assuming that it has been set up correctly, you only pay if the person searching decides to click on your advert – i.e. it has worked in attracting the attention of the viewer. Rates charged vary according to the popularity of the search terms governed by a system of "bidding" – so if the search term is popular, there will be others who are also trying to attract customers for that search term, so you bid against them to get your advert placed instead of theirs, and therefore may pay more per click. But all of this is automated – you just set the limit you are prepared to pay per click – say £0.90p – and the system automatically works out the bids.
- Easily controlled – once everything is set up, you can turn your advertising on and off instantaneously, which is a very useful facility for the private practitioner who

may only wish to top-up the amount of clients without committing to a set expenditure. Other control mechanisms include being able to set:

- o The geographical reach of your advert
- o The amount you spend per day
- o The days of the week, and the times of day your advert appears
- Easily monitored using the built-in reports that show the number of clicks, the adverts that are working the best (you can have more than one running simultaneously), the efficiency of each advert in terms of how many times it appears ("impressions") against the amount of times it is clicked as a result, known as the "click through rate"
- Almost instantaneous in set up, and not requiring any special software – just an internet connections and a credit card!

It has also proved very cost effective. As stated in my conversation with Arthur above, I know that I get about 1 new client for every £20 I spend on Google AdWords (that's about 15 clicks), and the efficiency of this could probably be improved by making ever greater efforts to improve the amount of new clients I get for the amount of visitors to my site (known as "conversion rate" in web-speak).

Once you have a website up, we consider this sort of promotional activity an absolute must.

Online directories

Providing they are carefully chosen, online directories such as www.counsellingdirectory.co.uk or the BACP's own online list of members are useful ways of getting additional referrals.

The benefits are twofold:

1. Firstly, directory companies focus heavily on being really easy to find – they have to in order to be successful. Consequently, they put a lot of effort into promoting their sites, and employ specialists to stay up-to-date with the way in which search engines work. So by paying to be listed on a good counselling directory means that you are improving your chances of being found by potential clients.

2. Secondly, Google uses special software to "score" your website in terms of relevance. This scoring determines how high on the natural listings ("natural" listings are the main, non-paid-for search results) your website link will appear. Get it right, and your website could be at the top of the natural listing, have an advert on page 1, and be linked to by other sites like directories – all of which give the viewer a distinct impression that your service is highly relevant and professional.

Once you have a website up, we consider this sort of promotional activity a valuable investment. But make sure you work *with* the advertiser to get the best out of your investment.

Social media

Visit almost any company website these days and you will see icons for Facebook, LinkedIn, Twitter and any one of a number of other social media channels. For many companies, these services offer another way of engaging with customers, but for counselling social media is not appropriate.

The clue to the problem is in the title – social. Ask yourself this – how would a man feel about following an "Erectile Dysfunction Support Group" on Facebook where their Facebook page is visible to others in that persons' social community. Following Twitter contributors face similar challenges.

Social media is used by corporations to *evangelise* products by creating interesting content that is likely to be shared by individuals on their own FaceBook or similar pages. For example, I follow Mercedes-Benz on FaceBook because I like their cars and their Formula-1 team. When interesting content is posted by Mercedes-Benz, I might "like" or "share" that content, or "comment" on it – when I do this, everyone else in my social circle gets to see, and so the message about the brand spreads.

Social media is also used to help corporations monitor a brands' health, watching what people are saying about brands and, if they're good, quickly respond and resolve issues that crop up. Huge corporations have been brought to their knees by unmonitored, unresolved disputes that have been shared and spread rapidly through the Internet.

One area that might be of interest is Blogs. Web-Logs (bLogs) are online published written content open to everyone. You can use standard, free software to do this (e.g. WordPress) and can link them to your own website. This can be a useful way of demonstrating that you are knowledgeable about your niche subject area, but there are pitfalls. One major concern for Counsellors is in how easy it is to shift the balance of power by making you the authority and not the client. Or writing statements that can be sweeping or misinterpreted by sensitive clients.

It may be pertinent to larger organisations with a broader appeal and the resources required to keep a page up to date and interesting, but it is unlikely to be of interest to the private practitioner. And unless you're an accomplished writer, able to carefully convey the meaning of your thoughts, Blogs may well take up a lot of time and yield little, nothing or even negative results.

Summary

Lets put these activities into a priority list, and grouped into "must", "preferable", "avoid" and "Not appropriate".

1. Website	Must haves
2. Online advertising	
3. Business cards and brochures	Preferable
4. Online directories	
5. Printed directories	Avoid
6. Print advertising	
7. Social Media	Not appropriate
8. Flyers and special promotions	
9. Email marketing and list rental	

Making a website work for you – a step-by-step guide

Building a website can be as complicated as boiling an egg – if you don't know how to go about it, if you don't understand the mechanisms that are essential for it to work, it's complicated. But like boiling an egg, we can learn what we need to learn to complete the task.

The question of how to build a website, and more importantly how to build a website that works, is the perennial question of Counsellors. Unless you have a background in website design, it is likely to be a minefield of terminology that you do not understand, and we always fear what we don't understand.

In this chapter, we will give you the basics of what you need to know to make a website work for you.

<u>*Where to start*</u>

First, lets remind ourselves as to what your website needs to achieve from the work we did previously through the acronym AIDCA. We can think of it in the following equation:

Visitors to the site

X

Conversion rate of visitors into clients

=

Clients generated

It's the same formula for any business. A coffee shop's profits are determined by the number of visitors to the coffee shop multiplied by the shops' ability to convert those visitors into customers (by having good coffee, a speedy service and the capacity to up-sell a pastry or a delicious blueberry muffin).

So for your website, we need to think in terms of:

1. Attracting customers to your website by making it easy to find and relevant to their needs/pain
2. The design of a website to quickly confirm its relevance to them, and its ability to generate confidence in you and your service, and then making it simple to take action and get in touch

It is crucial to think of websites in this way because it helps us separate out the jobs that are required, and to keep us focused on what is important. But first, lets demystify website design by walking you through the various stages of publishing a website.

Website design has spawned a mindboggling amount of terminology that leaves most of us completely confused. So the first job of this chapter is to help break down website design into its constituent parts, and to explain the terminology that is relevant to you being able to commission a website yourself. Then we will look at the four different ways of getting on the web.

Stage 1 – Setting up

As you begin to develop a website, there are some basic things that need to be organised before you start designing.

Firstly, complete the "Finding your niche" workshop, as this will determine everything else, the name of your service, the style of language used, photography choices and any relevant sections that should be included.

Once this is complete, you can then purchase a Domain Name. A Domain Name is the website's address, e.g. www.microsoft.com, www.bbc.co.uk or www.marksandspencer.co.uk, and appears at the top of your web browser (the program on your computer that you use to browse the Internet, e.g. Microsoft's Explorer or Apple's Safari)

Domain Names have different endings. The examples above are the international company designation ".com" and the UK specific company designation ".co.uk". There are many others including ".org" (often charitable organisations), ".net", ".me", ".uk.com" etc. – the choice you make helps the viewer (and Search Engines like Google) to determine how to categorise you. If you're a UK based Counsellor, we would suggest you purchase a ".co.uk" Domain Name.

When you come to register, you might find that your choice is already taken. Perhaps you choose to call yourself "Glasgow Counselling for Couples" but discover that www.glasgowcounsellingforcouples.co.uk is already taken. This simply means that someone else has already registered that Domain Name – it does not mean that they have a site up and running, or that they even intend to – sometimes Domain Names are purchased to prevent others from having them, or by so-called "Cyber Squatters" who buy names they think will be popular and then attempt to sell them onto you at a profit. The simple way to get around this is to either select a different ending to the domain name (e.g. ".com" or ".uk.com") or by trying a different permutation of the Domain Name, for example:

www.glasgowcouplecounselling.co.uk

    or

www.couplecounsellinginglasgow.co.uk

Domain Names cost about £10 for 2 years, and you can buy them online at registration companies like www.123reg.co.uk. They will then register the site with the Domain Name registration service NOMINET.

Stage 2 – Organising content into pages

Without getting too distracted for now with layout and design features, organise your thoughts into specific pages. Use a simple pad and pen, or perhaps a word processor on a computer – anything you're comfortable with. Start a new piece of paper for each web page, put a title at the top of the page and make notes about what the page is meant to achieve.

There are three pages that are common to most websites, and then you have some freedom to decide on some additional pages.

Websites always have a "Home" page. This page is the first page of a website and is used as the default page for visitors and frequently used by Search Engines as they seek to classify your site. The home page can be thought of the tree trunk from where other branches stem. The home page should welcome viewers, be compelling enough for viewers to stop and read and go further into your site. (This is known as "stickiness" in the trade – remember how easy it is to click onto and off of a website – creating a sticky site that captures the attention of visitors so that they do not simply click away is crucial if you are to keep them long enough to convert them into clients.)

We would also suggest that an "About Me" page should be included, with a photograph of yourself, so that potential clients get to read about you. I have found that by including a simple photograph of myself in a t-shirt, deliberately showing part of my tattoo, clients have said how reassuring it was to discover that I was just another guy – which was part of my niche objectives. This page may also be a good place to tell clients where you are based and how much you charge, although you may choose to do this on a separate page.

You should *always* have an action page (see AIDCA) where telephone numbers, email contact details and/or an email "Form" (a web designers term for common repeat elements where viewers can enter details) can be placed to help visitors get in touch with you.

Now you should add a few additional pages to your site. These are useful for writing about specific examples or common complaints for your subgroup, as determined during Workshop 2 – Finding your Niche. The primary reason to do this is to provide you with some specific issues that you can use as the focus of specific advertising campaigns (we're going to cover this later under "Generating Volume" below). They are also very helpful in creating confidence in your clients that you know what you're talking about.

Once you have finished organising your content into pages, you can create an index. Most websites have a repeated element, typically at the top or the left hand side, where "Navigation buttons" are included so that the visitor can easily skip around your site and find what they are looking for. The pages are the branches of the tree, denoted by including a "forward slash" ("/"), e.g. www.domainname.co.uk/aboutme or www.domainname.co.uk/contactus

Think carefully about the content. Don't overwhelm your visitors with pages or content – 6 or 7 pages maximum we would suggest, and leave them hungry for more content and encourage them to get in touch for more information. Use the niche exercise in Workshop 2 to help you determine the language that you're seeking to use, and make it as easy as possible for visitors to get the information they need quickly by using meaningful photographs, diagrams, lists, bullet points and headings.

Stage 3 - Design

What is good design? Is it the correct use of colours, font choice, funky features that zoom in and out or play a tune? If we remember where we started on this chapter, we are reminded that the only thing that is important when it comes to web design is to convert visitors into clients. Consequently, good design is a design that is good at assisting this conversion, not necessarily a design that looks good.

Principal 9 – Aesthetics are not important. Conversion rate is the only thing that matters

Indeed, some design features on websites are really off-putting and inappropriate for an audience that is typically suffering. We would suggest that less-is-more with website design, using lots of blank space to separate out content, making text easier to read, and thinking about placement of text, photographs and other elements to draw the eye of the visitor to help them consume your content.

The old adage "a picture paints a thousand words" is pertinent for website design. However, it is a complete mistake to use pictures that say nothing or are easily misinterpreted. We see a lot of websites that use pseudo-spiritual tokens like standing stones or pebbles balanced one of top of another. Images such as these are at best meaningless, and at worst misinterpreted as a Buddhist metaphor – fine if this fits with the niche that you have identified for yourself, but off-putting to those who might have strong opinions about religion.

The best pictures to use are those that include us – humans. They convey relevance to visitors because well-chosen photographs of people convey the emotions or situation that these potential clients find themselves. Our human brains are amazingly adept at spotting emotion from a picture, even a picture of nothing other than the human eye. Use this capacity and choose photographs that paint emotions that work to support the content of your webpages – we suggest one photograph per page so as to avoid the page becoming cluttered with images.

Good quality photography is easier to find than you might think. Marketers use Stock Photography image banks. Take a look at www.shutterstock.com or www.istockphoto.com. Use the built-in search engines to find just the right photograph and then download that image to your computer.

We strongly recommend this method of getting photographs as it ensures that you are legally using the images and not in danger of copyright infringement by using someone else's images. They are not expensive – just a few pounds ranging up to no more than £30 or £40 for large images – which is a lot less than being sued! If you want to download a test image before programming, most stock photography banks have images called "comp" or "comping" images that are marked in a way that makes them un-publishable, but are good enough for testing/layout purposes.

Finally, remember to download the larger versions of your images if you plan to use them in any printed items (business cards, brochures etc.), as print media requires high-resolution photography. All Windows and Mac computers have free built in software that can be used to scale large photographs down to a smaller, web-friendly size, but you cannot scale up photographs without making them look grainy.

Stage 4 – Page identifiers

Search engines like Google use special software called "Spiders" that reach into each page of your website in order to understand what your webpage is all about. These Spiders then store this information and it becomes part of Google's huge database of information that is then made available to the world.

An important part of this categorisation and ranking is the way in which everything about your webpage is organised to repeat and confirm words that are relevant to that site. So, the title, the headings, the text, and the names of the photographs used should all be deliberately repeated in order to confirm the subject of each individual page to the Spider.

Web designers also deliberately help Spiders by providing a small hidden area at the beginning of each web page where the Spider is invited to look. This area includes a special list of words known as "Meta-Tags" which are words that the web developer would prefer the Spider to use as its indexing.

So re-read each page of content and create a list of 10-20 key words that you would like Google to refer to – words like "counselling", "therapy", "depression" etc.

Stage 5 – The 4 different ways of getting on the web

By now, you should have a Domain Name, page names and headings, content, an index, supporting photography and Meta-Tags for each webpage. You have spent no more than £50-£100 on Domain Names and Photographs. You might have developed an idea of how you would like your content to appear on the Internet, so now you have four different methods of getting your notepad based ideas programmed into web pages and published.

Each of these methods has pro's and con's, but essentially they all require two processes – programming the content into web pages, and then uploading the content to a special computer called a "Server" operated by a website hosting company (often called an Internet Service Provider or ISP).

1. The first method is to **pay a web designer to develop something for you**. The great advantage of this is that web developers know what they are doing and can get a good looking site uploaded rapidly. The main disadvantage is cost – be prepared to pay between £500 and £1500 for a website company to develop a site for you, and be prepared for them to charge you each time you wish to make alterations to your text. Such companies will typically look after the uploading of your website content to a hosting Server, and may also offer to host (or organising hosting on your behalf) at an extra cost.
2. The second method is to use a **template design & hosting company** like www.webhealer.net. You need very little computer knowledge, and simply choose a design from one of the many different design templates available and then follow the instructions for uploading your

text and photographs to the site. The great advantage is that they look after everything else making this a very simple solution. The biggest disadvantage is that you are limited to the designs that they have available, but the amount of design and the level of customisation available makes this the least complicated, fastest and most reliable means of getting online.

3. Thirdly, there are companies like www.reg123.co.uk that will sell you a Domain Name, provide you with free *online software and website hosting all in one*. The software is a type known as What-You-See-Is-What-You-Get (WYSIWYG) that gives you a reasonable amount of customisation and technical support. The disadvantages with this method are the level of computer skill required, and the relatively limited design alternatives.

4. Finally, you can *buy your own website design software* such as Flux or Serif WebPlus or even the top-of-the-range DreamWeaver and do the job yourself. While this clearly requires a huge learning curve on your part, it can work out the best long-term as it gives you the flexibility to make any amount of alterations and any number of other websites.

Summary of typical costs

Below we have collated an estimate of what is typically charged for the various elements of developing and hosting a website so as to help you avoid being overcharged:

- Domain Name purchase £10, renewable annually
- Option 1 – Web company design services for a 5-7 page website - £500 - £1000 with agreed service charges for nominal updates
- Option 2 – Template hosting (eg www.webhealer.net) - £40-£450 set up, then £14-£24 per month
- Option 3 – WYSIWYG software, e.g. Wix (£varies)
- Option 4 – buy software, e.g. Flux (£90), Serif WebPlus etc.

Generating online volume

Once you have your website up and running, the next stage will be making your website easy to find so that potential clients can read what you have to offer and make contact with you for an initial appointment.

We have already discussed a range of promotional techniques that you might consider for this, but we are going to concentrate on getting your website visible through Google. This is done in two parts – Search Engine Optimisation and AdWords.

Search Engine Optimisation (SEO)

Search Engine Optimisation is the process of helping your website get ranked as high as possible in Google's Natural Listing search results (the non-advert results in Google). Search Engines have become so good that people expect to find what they are looking for very quickly, and tend not to scroll down even the first page of Google, let alone click forward to subsequent pages. Consequently, it has become critically important for websites to be ranked as high as possible in order that they appear in the top half of the natural search results.

SEO has become an industry all of its own, and you can expect to start getting phone calls from SEO companies almost as soon as your website is live on the Internet. While specialist SEO companies are useful for businesses that tend to be poorly differentiated (e.g. try searching for something like "toys" on Google and see how many results it returns – millions!), for specialist companies like counsellors, the job is relatively strait forward and you probably do not need SEO services.

If you have followed the previous instructions on developing Meta-Tags and have a clearly differentiated service, you are already halfway there. Google's "Spidering" software is very good at working out how well your website should be ranked for and given search. However, this can be helped by using tools that submit and re-submit the contents of your website constantly to a wide range of search engines. You might think of them as constantly waving at Search Engines, attracting the attention of Spiders and inviting them to re-Spider your site.

You will typically pay a small annual subscription for this service - £15-£30 a year depending on the level of service you decide on, but once your site has been favourably ranked, keeping it up is relatively simple.

The other thing that you can do for no cost at all is periodically modify the contents of each page on your website. It doesn't have to be much – add a paragraph, or change a photograph – the Google Spiders notice that something has changed and presumes that this means that your site is active and alive, improving the Ranking still further.

Google AdWords

AdWords is Google's own online advertising service. AdWords is responsible for a huge amount of profit for Google, and is very, very good. So good, in fact, that we listed it as a "must have" in our promotion summary above.

AdWords works by allowing you to choose and "bid" for search words (called "Key Words" in Google speak) so that when someone is searching on Google for, say, "relationship counselling" an advert for your relationship counselling service pops up at the side of the screen. However, you only pay anything when your advert is clicked (literally called "Pay Per Click"). The better your advert is at attracting just the right sort of potential customer, plus the better your website is at "converting" those visitors into enquiries, the better your AdWords work and the less you spend on AdWords to yield a paying client.

AdWords are run as Campaigns. You can have numerous adverts for each Campaign, enabling you to test which advert works best.

Once you have created a campaign and a selection of adverts, you tell/point the advert to the specific page on your website you would like the visitor to land. Normally, you would have a generic Campaign, landing the visitor on your home page. But you could also have sub-campaigns to attract specific types of clients. This is why in *Stage 2 – organising contents into pages* above we suggested having additional pages – if, say, your relationship counselling service offered an extra "preparation for marriage" coaching service that was a specific page on your website, say www.yourdomainname.co.uk/relationshipcoaching, you could run a complete sub-campaign for individuals who search specifically for this type of service, or even those who put "unsure of marriage" into Google!

Like natural listings, AdWords have a Rank too. Positions 1 & 2 typically appear above the natural listings on page 1 of Google's results, and positions 3-6 appear to the right of the natural listings. AdWords that Rank 7 and beyond are on subsequent pages of the Google search results, and given that people searching the internet for services rarely click beyond page 1 of the results, it is important that your adverts are ranked 1-6 to maximise results.

However, increasing your ranking is easy – simply increase the amount you are prepared to pay for each click – the "Bid" amount. Remember, you only pay when the advert is actually clicked. The efficiency of getting site visitors to convert to clients is the job of your website.

AdWords is also geographically selectable, i.e. you can tell AdWords that you only want your advert to appear on computers within a given radius of a specific postcode.   This is a very useful feature for the private practitioner who is not interested in attracting people from outside a reasonable geographical catchment area.

Google AdWords is free to set up. You will need to put some money "on account" with Google for them to draw off as your adverts are clicked, so a credit or debit card would be useful. Search for AdWords on Google and follow the instructions, or get in touch with **The *Business of Counselling*** for advice.

Summary

By continuously improving your adverts, key-words and website, you can gain ever higher efficiencies in "Click-through" and "Conversion" rates. For large companies that spend £millions with Google AdWords every year, there is a significant interest in making continuous improvements to the efficiency of this system, but for most private practitioners, getting to a level where £20 on AdWords yields one new client is still excellent value for money.

Principal 10 – Invest in ever better levels of marketing efficiency

The optimum position is to have a high natural ranking and a high AdWord ranking. By investing a little time and money in a good website, a sensible level of Search Engine Optimisations, and a small AdWords campaign, we believe that you'll soon have a healthy client list and a steady income.

Workshop B – finding your niche

Use this to help you determine your niche.

- Don't describe your service in terms of what you do, rather in terms of what your service does for your client.
- What "pain" does your service solve? What benefit does it bring to the client? What will they search for?
- Not "Counselling service" rather "a service to help you overcome problems with BLANK".
- Who is your client – How old are they? What gender are they? What problems do they typically present? What's close to your heart? What did/do you wish you could find as a specialism?
- Think of 3 or 4 different common complaints for this group to generate specific web pages

You can also have a "niche within a niche".

- Couples counselling = poor.
- Bradford Couples Counselling = good.
- Bradford Islamic Couples Counselling = better.

Section 3 – Accounting basics

The number one reason why businesses fail is not because of poor product, poor service or poor marketing, but because of a poor attention to the control and flow of money. As your private practice grows, so too will the amount you have to pay for the things required to keep it going – room rental, telephone and internet services, a computer and printer, stationary and other office consumables, supervision, liability insurance, bank charges, marketing, professional fees (e.g. BACP & an accountant, if required), etc. You will also enter the realm of needing to liaise directly with the Tax Man, declaring your earnings, justifying your business expenses, and paying Income Tax and National Insurance contributions.

But perhaps the biggest single pressure on any private practitioner is the *need* to make money. A bunny-in-headlights paralyzing fear frequently overwhelms those starting out, a fear that takes us back to the basics of Maslow's hierarchy of needs – the need for food, shelter and security. Put simply, your capacity to earn money and have enough money to feed you and the children (and put a little set aside for a rainy day) puts enormous pressures on getting this right. There have been a (thankfully small) number of high profile cases of mal-practice where individuals have abused the therapeutic relationship they have with their clients in order to get money. Or cases of therapists doing anything to avoid paying tax ending up in court charged with fraud. Even holding onto a client in order to retain income when that client should probably be released could be a reaction to this pressure.

If all of this sounds daunting, then don't worry – all you need to be able to do is add-up and stick to a list of simple processes explained in this section – we will provide you with a simple accounting system.

What you need to be able to do is:

1. Keep track of how much you have earned and spent
2. Keep track of who owes you how much, and show you how to generate invoices
3. Keep the tax man happy, and prepare you for paying tax and National Insurance
4. Provide you with a system that will satisfy the tax man, should he wish to inspect your business earnings
5. Sleep well at night!

The ultimate aim of being in business is to enable you to pay yourself a good "salary" for your hard work, rest well at night knowing that your operation is legal, profitable, and professional, and that there are no surprises waiting for you around the next corner!

Why have an accounting system?

The accounts department is a key fixture in any business. As stated under "Thinking like a Managing Director", this function is one of three that are key to all businesses. Before we move forward into answering "*how*" to run an accounting system, it is important that you understand "*why*" an accounting system is needed at all.

"*Why*" can be answered in three ways – to keep your business *Legal*, to provide *Control,* and to maintain a *Professional* appearance.

Legal

One of my previous employments was as a Public Relations manager for a large Indian IT Company. The company was listed on the Indian stock exchange and had many shareholder investors. It was the height of a time when the UK press was running headlines like "UK jobs going to India", when outsourcing was one of a number of reasons being blamed for a slow-down in the UK economy. This sort of scrutiny meant that my job was primarily keeping the company *out* of the newspapers, and seeking to ensure that it maintained a steady stream of positive reports based on solid results.

One day, I was sat with the CEO of the company, a very wealthy and well-respected man, and my ultimate boss. He was a man of simple means, not flaunting his wealth, but choosing to live a simple life. As we waited for a journalist to arrive for an interview, I tried to persuade him to talk to the journalist about a particular topic that he considered risky. I was keen for this story to be told as I believed it would help the company's image in the UK, but the CEO turned to me and spoke gently, raising a finger to emphasise his point, smiled and said, "The softest pillow is a clear conscience", and we agreed to hold off on that particular story until we had solid evidence.

This statement – "The softest pillow is a clear conscience" – has always stayed with me, and it is the single biggest reason why you, as a private practitioner, should adopt a simple accounting system – it keeps you legal and means that you can sleep well at night, safe in that knowledge.

Like most countries, the UK has a tax system that requires, under law, that you tell the Tax Man how much you have earned so that your tax liability (i.e. the amount of tax you owe) can be calculated and arrangements made for you to pay this. Failure to do so is fraud, a criminal offence that carries a custodial sentence. Gulp! An accounting system is, at its heart, *the* means for being able to provide *evidence* of your income and expenditure so as to enable you *to know and show* that what you are declaring as income is true.

Control

Most of us run our household accounts based on a system that can be best described as approximation, i.e. we roughly know what is coming-in and what is going-out every month. For most people, income is reasonably predictable (given that most people in the UK are paid weekly or monthly on a salaried basis), and most households can have a reasonable approximation of expenditure, using direct debit facilities to spread out larger bills over a 12 month period.

For a business, this is not adequate enough. Businesses need to be able to monitor expenditure accurately, and to know who owes you how much. Imagine a time when you have 20 clients in a week – a simple but reliable system for tracking who has seen you and when, how much money has been collected and in what method of payment, and who owes you money "on account" to be invoiced at the end of each month is crucial. Failure to have this recorded accurately means potential lost income, or over- or under-charging clients.

An accounting system is also the means by which you prove your income. If, for instance, you wished to raise a mortgage, you would need to provide the lending bank with proof of your earnings. A simple accounting system would certainly help to show the bank that you are worth the risk, as well as showing them that you know what you're doing.

Professional

Cash is a nightmare for the Tax Man. Cash is a "liquid" method of transaction, i.e. cash can be received and spent again on almost anything without that cash ever being declared as income to the Tax Man. This _Black Market_ is huge, and it enables unscrupulous traders to dodge paying tax on income and dodge VAT. The difficulties of tracing and prosecuting offenders of this sort of fraud means it has become pseudo-normal in society in a similar way to motorway speed limits – "everyone does it occasionally, so it's ok".

Your clients are expecting a professional service, and, with so many private practitioners frequently taking payment in cash from clients, the opportunity for clients to presume that this money is not being declared is an opportunity for the client to presume that your service is not professional.

An accounting system records everything in and everything out. If a new client is given the freedom to choose between cash, cheque, card payment, or bank transfer, and they are provided each month with either a statement of account and/or an invoice, then this ambiguity is eliminated.

By doing so, it eliminates the possibility of misinterpretation of your professionalism, and makes charging for missed sessions or late-cancelled sessions much more enforceable.

Some business basics

Having established *why* an accounting system is needs, it is now time to move onto the nuts and bolts of *how* that system will work. First, we will answer some basic questions about setting up a business, as these will lay the foundations for understanding the next steps.

Introducing Bob. How to conceptualise your business

One of the most confusing aspects of accounting is a simple one of how a business is conceptualised.

Your business is not you. Your business needs to be thought of as an individual entity in its own right. This way, your clients do not pay you, they pay the business. The business pays its business bills, and the money in the business belongs to the business, not you. It only becomes your money when the business pays you a salary/wage/dividend and money is transferred from the business to you.

By keeping you and your business' financial affairs separate, you greatly simplify the way in which your accounts can be compiled. This makes it clear what is yours and what is the company's, what you have paid yourself as a wage (and therefore what you should be taxed on), and makes it really easy to demonstrate what has been bought on your behalf by the company (like a computer), and, were the Tax Man to ask to look (which he can legally demand to do at any time), it would demonstrate to him that you are running your affairs with clarity.

It might help to give you business a name – let's call it Bob. You work as a counsellor for Bob. A client gives you money for counselling services and you pay it into Bob's bank account (in this way, you are a cashier, taking money and putting it in the till). Bob pays for all the business expenses – the room rental, telephone and internet services, a computer and printer, stationary and other office consumables, supervision, liability insurance, bank charges, marketing, professional fees (e.g. BACP & an accountant, if required), and payments on any loans. Bob then pays you a salary and that money is the money that you then declare on your personal tax return.

Bob might also provide you with a car for your use to get to and from clients, but because you would have both personal and business use of this car, it is classed by the Tax Man as a "benefit in kind" and you would be charged some tax for it on your personal tax liability.

If you work from home, Bob might also "rent" that room from you and pay a contribution towards your heating & electricity bills.

Be aware that Bob might also have to pay tax. Any profit that Bob makes (profit being the amount of money left over in Bob's account after everything has been paid for) is also typically liable to an annual business or corporation tax, which are typically lower than those of individual taxation.

This sounds confusing at first, but it is a simple way of keeping your personal accounts (with your personal tax liability) separate from your business accounts (with its own different tax liabilities where applicable).

A note about insurance

Limited companies have limited liability. That literally means that the liability any limited company has is, well, limited! A sole trader, on the other hand, has unlimited liability.

In fact, this is not entirely accurate. The truth is that if someone who has received your services believes so strongly that you have damaged them by your actions / inactions / malpractice etc., then you can be sued through the civil courts regardless of your company status.

You should, therefore, get insurance. It's not expensive, and if you're a BACP or UKCP member, there are schemes available through these organisations to give you a good level of cover for your practice. Towergate (www.towergate.co.uk) have a long association with the BACP, and will provide you with £1million worth of cover plus legal expenses for £100-£200 per year.

If you work from home, you should also include some personal injury cover in case a client trips over your rug, falls down the stairs or breaks the toilet! However, if you rent an office, such cover is probably the responsibility of the landlord, not you. But check.

VAT in the UK

Value Added Tax (VAT) is an additional tax levied by the UK Government on products and services. Currently VAT stands at 20% - so a client session fee of £40 would have a VAT charge of £8 per session, making the total fee chargeable to a client £48.

The extra £8 is not great for the client, and the collection and payment of VAT to the Tax Man is an administrative headache for you. (When a business is registered for VAT, it effectively becomes a tax collector, saving up the numerous £8's and paying them to the Tax Man on a quarterly basis.) There are some benefits to traders of being VAT registered, but for the small trader, it is probably more trouble than it is worth.

The good news is that, providing your business does not reach a specific level of income per year (called the VAT Threshold), then your business does not need to charge VAT and you do not need to register for VAT. Currently, this threshold is £85,000 per year (April 2017). At a client fee of £40 per session, you would need to see 34 clients a week to exceed this level. At a client fee of £50 per session, you would need to see 27 clients a week to exceed this level. At a client fee of £60 per session, you would need to see 23 clients a week to exceed this level. Consequently, we do not anticipate that this will be a necessity for you as a private practitioner. Should your business get to the VAT threshold level, we would recommend you invest in some professional business advice from an accountant.

The accounting year

Tax is calculated on how much you earn in any given year. However, the Tax Man does not use the calendar year of January 1st to December 31st. Instead, the Tax Man uses April to March. The historic reasons for this are simply that this was once considered to be New Year in the way that we think of January 1st as being New Year now.

Individual tax liability falls within this period, i.e. you will need to pay the Tax Man your personal tax liability (not Bobs!) on money earned between April and March of the following calendar year. (Actually, the new tax year starts on April 6th and concludes on April 5th of the following year.)

In order to keep things simple, we would suggest that you set up your business' accounting year to also be April 1st to March 31st. In this way, you will be able to close your accounts on the business and on your personal liability at the same time.

This does not mean that you must wait until the next April 1st to start trading – you simply close your first year at the next March 31st having completed how ever many months of trading you have left in that financial year.

The Tax Return

As a self-employed individual, you will be required to complete and submit an annual Tax Return.

The Tax Return is a multi-part form where all you income is detailed. It contains space for you to list all of your income and any tax already paid. For example, you might be part-employed, part self-employed; you may have income from property rental or pensions, interest on savings or even an inheritance. All this income is declared to the Tax Man on this form, and the amount of tax you owe is then calculated.

When you start trading, you **must** register your self-employed status with the Tax Man and he will ensure that you get sent reminders and all the necessary information to complete your tax return on time. It is a criminal offence to not do so.

At the end of the personal tax year (March 31st), the Tax Man will write to you and tell you that you have up until January 31st of the following year to complete and file your tax return, and pay any tax owed. So, in January 2015, you would need to pay the tax you owe on income received between April 1st 2013 and March 31st 2014; in January 2016, you would need to pay the tax you owe on income received between April 1st 2014 and March 31st 2015, and so on.

All of this is now done online, including payments of tax owed, but make sure you do not leave it until the last minute, as there are numerous registration processes to go through before you can complete your filing.

We would strongly recommend that you save a little for your tax liability every month. My company (Bob) pays me at the end of each month, and I automatically transfer 1/3 of that into a separate personal savings account so that I have the money to pay the Tax Man when he requires it. 1/3rd is a large proportion, but I would rather have more than enough for the Tax Man, and anything left over is mine to keep (or spend on the summer holiday with my wife!)

Be aware that once you reach a threshold of £1000[5] per year in tax owed, you will be required to begin paying tax "on account" in anticipation of future tax liability. Up until this threshold, you have to make a single payment at the end of January for the tax owed on the previous financial year (as in the example above, paying the tax you owe on income received between April 1st 2013 and March 31st 2014 in January 2015).

---

[5] *Correct in 2012-13 tax year. But check the HMRC website for "Payments on Account" as this figure changes*

Once you cross this threshold, the Tax Man requires you to pay for the previous year as before, *AND* pay half as much again there-and-then as a first instalment of an anticipated tax liability for the current financial year – then in July, you would need to pay the other 50%, meaning that by the end of July, you have already theoretically paid your tax bill for that year (assuming your income does not change from one year to the next). I almost fainted when this happened to me because I had not read the small print and realised that this was required!

However, once you have broken into this way of paying your tax, by the time the next January comes round, you will have already paid your tax bill (assuming your income does not substantially change). So in that next January, you would once again pay 50% of the current years' tax bill (any increase or decrease would be added-on or subtracted-from this amount), with the other 50% instalment due in the July.

Lets illustrate this:

Tax year	Tax liability	Payment schedule
'12-'13	£3500	• £3500 due Jan 31st, 2014 in a single, one-off payment
'13-'14	£5000	• £5000 due for the '13-'14 tax year • Threshold crossed, so add 50% (£2500) "on account" in expectation of the '14-'15 tax liability being the same • **_Both are due Jan 31st, 2015 (£5000 + £2500 = £7500)_** • A further £2500 due July 31st, 2015 (the other 50%) "on account" in expectation of the '14-'15 tax liability being the same • = £5000 "on account" for '14-'15 tax year • Note: You have paid for last years' tax **_and_** this years expected tax liability in 1 year, in this example £10000! Gulp!
'14-'15	£5500	• £5500 is calculated as the actual tax liability for '14-'15 • But you have already paid £5000 "on account" towards this years' liability • Therefore, £5500 - £5000 = £500 underpayment for '14-'15 • Therefore, £500 + 50% of the expected liability for '15-'16 £2750 (50% of £5500) = £3250 due Jan 31st, 2016 • A further £2750 (50%) "on account" in expectation of the '15-'16 tax liability being the same due July 31st, 2016

Tax year	Tax liability	Payment schedule
'15-'16	£4800	• This year the actual tax liability for '15-'16 is less at £4800 • But you have already paid £2750+£2750=£5500 "on account" • Therefore, £4800 - £5500 = £700 overpayment for '15-'16 • Therefore, £-700 + 50% of the expected liability for '16-'17 £2400 (50% of £4800) = £1700 due Jan 31st, 2017 • A further £2400 (50%) "on account" in expectation of the '16-'17 tax liability being the same due July 31st, 2017

Do not try and deceive the Tax Man – he can legally demand to see all of your accounts (including any linked accounts, e.g. shared accounts with a spouse). Remember, "The softest pillow is a clear conscience" – pay Caesar what is Caesar's and sleep well at night!

We are not tax consultants – the illustrations here are simply taken from our experience. There are today many small tax accountants that will sort all of this for you for a small fee, typically £150-£500 depending upon the complexity of your tax calculations. This will be money well spent (especially as they are far more likely to know how to legally reduce your tax liability).

Personal Income Tax & National Insurance calculations

The calculation for personal taxation is not strait forward. Indeed, the complexity of the system is undoubtedly one of the main reasons why so many people avoid going into business in the first place, preferring instead to receive a salary with Income Tax and National Insurance (NI) already deducted (known as "Pay As You Earn" or PAYE).

HMRC continues to try and make the system as simple as possible, but it has inherited complexity that it inevitably makes taxation a headache. At the same time, we read almost daily stories of tax avoidance and people being handed jail terms for fraud, stories that instil fear into the minds of those who are approaching this subject for the first time. However, in all my dealing with HMRC they have been nothing but helpful and polite, and, provided there is no deliberate activity to defraud, generally seek to help you get it right. This section is designed to educate you and then give you a simple set of rules to follow to keep you on the right side of HMRC's rules.

We're going to attempt to explain the basics, but HMRC do a great job of helping you anticipate your tax and NI liability with this online ready-reckoner (https://www.gov.uk/self-assessment-ready-reckoner)

National Insurance

Let's deal with NI first. National Insurance comes in a number of "classes" that relate to your personal circumstances. All businesses, even your private practice, must pay Class 2 NI. But this is not a lot – currently a fixed rate of £2.85 per week.

As a Sole Trader, you will also have to pay Class 4 NI as part of your personal tax liability. This is calculated during your Self-Assessment tax return submission, and so does not require you to do anything special (other than make provision for it for payment!)

The calculation of what you pay for Class 4 is banded:

- Lower Profits Limit: If your annual earnings are less that £8164[6], you pay no Class 4.
- Upper Profits Limit: anything you earn above £8164 and up to £45000, you pay 9% Class 4. So, if you earned £30000, your Class 4 would be £30000-£8164=£21836 x 9% = £1965.24 (per annum)
- Anything you earn over the Upper Profits Limit is charged at 2%. So, if you earned £50000, your Class 4 would be £50000-£45000=£5000 x 2% = £100 PLUS £45000-£8164=£36836 x 9% = £3315.24, £100+£3315.24=£3415.24 (per annum)

Tax

UK tax has evolved in its designed over many, many years. Today, the system is deliberately biased towards placing the greatest burden of tax for the country on those who can most afford to pay, i.e. those who earn the most should pay the most tax. This means that those who earn the least pay proportionally less tax than those who earn lots and can therefore afford to pay a greater proportion of their income in tax.

To achieve this, UK tax is broken down into different levels, or bands. These different bands are directly associated with earnings – earn less than the lowest band and you pay no tax at all; earn more than that band, and you pay proportionally more tax. Currently, there are 4 bands of tax for individuals in the UK.

The first level is a "personal allowance". This is an amount of money that you can earn in a year and pay no tax. You may well have received a "Coding Notice" from HMRC in the past with your Tax Code – this code tells you how much you can earn before you start paying tax. For example, if your code is 875H, it means you can earn £8,750 per year without paying any tax at all. This coding

---

[6] *Correct as of May 2017*

changes periodically to reflect either small variations in the amount of tax you have under- or over-paid, or to reflect changes in your personal circumstances such as being married (under current rules, married couples receive a small tax benefit).

The next level is the "basic tax rate" level, currently set at 20%. This means that anything you earn over your personal allowance and up to the next threshold is taxed at 20%.

The next level is a 40% tax level for anything earned over £45,000, and finally there is a 50% tax rate for those earning over £150,000 per annum.

Lets illustrate this. In this example, the individual is earning £50,000 per annum, and has a tax code of 875H. S/he would pay tax calculated as below:

Tax band	Taxable amount	Tax rate	Tax to pay
Personal allowance	First £8,750	0%	£0
Basic rate	£45,000 - £8,750 = £36,250	20% tax	£7,250
Upper rate	£50,000- £45,000=£5000	40% tax	£2,000
Top rate	Nothing earned over £150,000	50% tax	£0
		Total	£9,250

In the following second example, the individual is earning £38,000 per annum, and has a tax code of 905B. S/he would pay tax calculated as below:

Tax band	Taxable amount	Tax rate	Tax to pay
Personal allowance	First £9,050	0%	£0
Basic rate	£38,000 - £9,050 = £28,950	20% tax	£5,790
Upper rate	Nothing earned over £45,000	40% tax	£0
Top rate	Nothing earned over £150,000	50% tax	£0
		Total	£5,750

Bank Accounts

The simple way of keeping the business and your own finances separate is to have a separate bank account for your business. This way, you can easily ensure that everything that belongs to the business is paid into the business or paid for by the business, and is ring-fenced away from your personal account(s).

The alternative is unthinkably complicated. Paying everything into and out of your own personal account, mixing it up with your grocery shopping and mortgage bills makes accounting very complicated. Was that £20 you received nine months ago a birthday gift from an affectionate aunt, or was it a payment from a client? Was that purchase at WHSmiths for me or for the business? And exactly how much have I earned from my work this year?

A separate account is highly advisable. The monthly bank statement provided by your bank *then becomes* the balance sheet of the company, helping you clearly demonstrate what is yours and what belongs to the business. It typically also means you have an extra debit card, making it easy to know when making a purchase whether that purchase is for the business of for you. This technique gives me absolute confidence that that purchase was a business purchase, even if I cannot immediately remember what it was for. And if I keep receipts of all such purchases (which we would recommend that you do), then I can quickly demonstrate what was purchased and why.

Most high street banks provide free "personal" banks accounts, i.e. accounts that do not have any bank charges levied and are designed to be used by an individual. If, however, you are running a business, banks would prefer you to use a designated business banking account. However, if you're intending to set yourself up as a sole trader you do not *need* a business bank account, and if you do not use too many cheques or counter services (which cost the bank money), then you're probably going to escape scrutiny.

The downside of a business bank account is that they are not free. Instead, typically a monthly fee is charged just to operate the account, and a small charge is also made for each cheque that you process. And all these charges add up.

Taking money

There are two ways of charging clients and four different ways of taking money from clients, each with its own benefits and pitfalls. Below is a table summarising the different charging and collection techniques, and an indication of how common they are:

	Cash	Cheque	Credit/debit card	Electronic transfer
Pay-as-you-go or pay per session	Common	Uncommon	Common	Common
Charge to account	Uncommon	Uncommon	Uncommon	Common

Charging: Pay-as-you-go vs. on-account

There are essentially two ways of charging your clients; you can either ask them to pay-as-you-go, paying for each session at the end of each session; or you can charge them "on account", keeping a tally of the amount of sessions they have attended per month and then sending them an invoice to be settled by them within a given time frame.

Pay-as-you-go is, perhaps, the simplest method for the private practitioner, and seems to be the favoured method for most clients. The key benefit of this system for you and the client is its simplicity – there is no need to keep track of money owed and money paid – you simply collect the cash of execute the credit card transaction there and then at the end of each session.

However, pay-as-you-go also has its complications, chief among which is the way in which it invites clients to not turn up and therefore not pay. If, like most practitioners, you insist on charging for last minute cancellations or did-not-attend ("DNA's) appointments, then collecting for these missed sessions can be difficult. It may even result in an abrupt ending to the work with the client, and leave you out of pocket, not to mention being very much a "bad ending".

Much of this can be avoided by having a tight, clearly boundaried (and enforced) contract, and we have heard of numerous techniques operated by some practitioners to aid collecting missed payments, including keeping credit card details "on file" and charging that card when a session is missed, or by charging a session in advance (so the client pays for the next session at the current session).

For the client, too, the pay-as-you-go model can unwittingly introduce difficulties in the therapeutic relationship. Pay-as-you-go might leave some feeling that the relationship is only as good as the next session. Or perhaps it could be interpreted as a dip-in, dip-out service that they can use when the psychological heat is especially high.

For clients that are likely to benefit from long-term work, issuing a monthly invoice (that includes missed appointments) avoids all this. This method involves keeping a record of when individuals attend, how much they owe, how much they have paid, sending out invoices and potentially chasing them for late payment. While the administration of this is a bit more involved, it is also a much more professional way of operating. And the Tax Man likes this method as it introduces a paper trail that can easily be verified. The client, too, is more likely to see this as professionalism, and it mitigates the possibility of the client mistakenly thinking that all you are interested in is the collection of your fee at the end of a session.

Apart from the administrative complications that this technique introduces, the biggest issue for the private practitioner is the delay between work done and fee collected. If your invoice asks for payment by the end of the following month, it is possible for fees to be owed for 7 or 8 weeks before they are collected. This delay can mean that you have more going out before you have it coming in, a common cash-flow[7] issue that can sink businesses if it is not properly managed. (See **Getting underway – forecasting & creating a positive cash flow** for more).

In practice, and in keeping with most service businesses, it makes sense to make provision for clients to choose a method that suits them and the way they run their own finances. This will almost certainly mean that you will have both systems running in parallel, albeit with a preference for one method over another.

Additionally the for the therapist, there are some interesting observations about the clients behaviour over payment that can be a useful input into the sessions, e.g. if a client pays you in advance might it be a communication of expectation for you to solve a problem, or if a client is repeatedly late in payment perhaps indicates an aggression towards you? All "grist for the mill" to be thought about with your supervisors!

Collecting by Cash

The most obvious collection method is cash. In our experience, cash is the preferred method of payment by clients on the pay-as-you-go system. But it has a few challenging issues.

The key issue is one of traceability. The Tax Man dislikes cash transactions, as it is all too easy to not declare cash income and stuff the money into a back pocket. This black-market of untraced, and untaxed transactions is rife and is likely to still be common

---

[7] *"Cash-flow" refers to the flow of money in and out of your business. Having a "positive cash-flow" simply means having enough money in the bank to ensure that you can pay your bills even if your income (those paying you) is delayed. Conversely, having a "negative cash-flow" means being in the frightening position of being owed money, but not actually having enough in the bank to pay what you owe.*

practice amongst poorly regulated business sectors. While you may vociferously protest otherwise, some clients may think that this is the way you operate. Do your clients believe that they are doing you a favour by paying you in cash (nudge, nudge, wink, wink!)?

This can easily be dispelled by issuing receipts and/or statements of account at the end of every month, something that the Tax Man will also approve of (see Receipts and Statement of Account below).

Another issue related to this is the way in which cash can infer a lack of value of your service in the mind of the client. I once had a taxi driver who paid me in cash, and it became quickly apparent that the cash he paid me with was cash he had no intention of declaring to the Tax Man himself, and it raised important questions about how he valued the work we were doing.

Withdrawing cash from the cash-point before each session can also result in missed payment or delayed starts for the disorganised client.

Collecting by Cheque

Personal cheques were once a popular non-cash transaction method, but they have fallen out of popularity and now almost completely fallen out of use.

A few years ago, banks withdrew the cheque guarantee scheme, removing the confidence traders once enjoyed that a cheque written for up to the value of £50 would be guaranteed by the bank regardless of the customers personal financial situation – if the bank issued a cheque book and guarantee card, they carried this risk. Today, if you accept a cheque and it bounces, the bank will send you the bounced cheque and it will become your responsibility to chase that person for some other means of settling the fee. Consequently, most high-street traders no longer accept cheques.

Cheques also have associated processing costs, often requiring manual entry into what has become a computerised system. If you use a business bank account, your bank is likely to charge you a fee for each cheque to cover this processing cost.

Banks are increasingly making cheques more and more unpopular for traders, and it is likely that they will simple cease to exist in due course. However, I our experience they are still occasionally used by clients to settle bills. But with transaction costs for cheques likely to increase, and the risk of loss of revenue (and associated chasing costs and administrative headache!) you may decide to follow the example on the high-street and simply not accept cheques at all.

Collecting by credit/debit card

Many transactions today are done via credit or debit cards. For banks, this is the dream ticket; pushing transactions onto computers removes the cost of human processing; accounts can be instantly checked to ensure that funds are available; security measures have made it very difficult for fraud to take place; banks are more likely to make money through interest payments charged on credit accounts; and banks charge a small processing fee on card transactions to trader.

This last point is worth being well informed about. A transaction fee of 2.75% on a £40 counselling session is £1.10. Providers justify this fee because they argue that it removes other costs involved in processing cash such as security, fraud or accounting staff required to count and process cash. For the small trader, including the private practitioner, this argument is irrelevant. Even for the likes of ASDA or Tesco, this argument is a bit weak as they still have to make provision for cash transactions. This fee could be added onto a transaction for client, but this would require them to pay the extra £1.10 per session. Alternatively, you could do as most traders do and swallow the fee as a necessary evil of trading.

There are a number of ways of taking card payments from customers. The first port of call is your bank who will be able to supply you with a credit card machine. However, these solutions are expensive – they require you to have a telephone connection, and banks will typically charge a setup fee, a rental fee for the machine and a transaction fee for each transaction. This is fine for the larger traders, but is prohibitively expensive for the small trader.

If you have an internet connection in your office and a computer to hand, or a smartphone with an app, you could look at PayPal (www.paypal.com) or similar online services. These services do not require you to have a box at home, rather simply take the card details and process the payment via the internet between client and you. You will be charged a transaction fee, but the service is free other than this charge. And the bill payer does not need to have a PayPal account to use this system.

There are also numerous smartphone/app powered services – check your app store for more.

The complexity and fees might lead you to conclude that this is to be avoided. Indeed, a quick poll of the private practitioners in our area shows that very few have card processing facilities. However, the main reason to embrace this technology is your clients – we are all so familiar with conducting transactions by card that not having card processing facilities seems almost antiquated. It is our view that card processing will rapidly become the norm, and will need to be integrated into your practice sooner rather than later.

Collecting by bank transfer

For those who are familiar with online banking, electronic transfer of funds is very simple and very efficient. And free. By providing your clients with you bank account and sort code numbers, you make it possible for them to rapidly transfer funds, and is becoming more and more popular a way of settling monthly invoices for counselling fees.

The biggest single headache of this system is that, until you go and check your bank statement, you have no idea that you have been paid, an issue that can lead to confusion. This could, of course, be mitigated by regularly checking your account, but this is laborious, especially if it requires you to log on via a computer. Increasingly, high-street banks are providing excellent mobile phone applications that enable you to perform simple checks like this from an iPhone or Android device.

Bookkeeping made (very) easy

Keeping track of who has paid you what, how much is owed to you, who is overdue with their payments, what you have paid out and how much money you have in the bank can sound overwhelming, especially for those who struggle with numbers and maths. But it does not need to be complicated.

Bookkeeping is a specific role undertaken by professionals known as "accounting technicians". These professionals know a great deal about how companies run their books, how to do audit checks, how to compile financial reports, and how to spot & prevent fraud. They are at the front line of running the business, generating invoices, paying bills, keeping track of petty cash and ensuring that receipts are organised properly. But you only need a fraction of this in order to get yourself underway.

What is important to the private practitioner is keeping a simple record of who owes you what and who has paid you what. The simple way to do this is to create a "Takings Journal", with each week having a separate sheet, collected together into a 52-page book for the entire year. Each sheet is connected to the previous and the next through balances that are carried forward from one week to the next.

The example below shows one week's entry for a fictional private practice that we will now go through to explain the system we propose you adopt. See Appendix 1 for the full sheet.

Column 1 records the date of the appointment. Column 2 records the name or identifier for the client. Column 3 records how much the client was charged. Columns 4, 5 & 6 records the money received from the client, and splits out cash, cheques and transfers (which would include credit card and bank transfer payments)

Each week's entry is linked to the previous and following week using the Opening and Closing balance columns. The Closing balance from the previous week is written in as the Opening balance (column 7) in this week's entry, and the Closing balance (column 8) from this week's sheet will become the Opening balance in next week's sheet. This mechanism is critical to keep a track of who owes how much.

The final two columns, columns 9 & 10, keep a handy record of outstanding amounts owed by clients who have been sent invoices.

Then at the bottom of the sheet, there is an area for recording summaries for the week and any pertinent notes. We also include here a running total of annual turnover, and a simple record of how much cash and cheques was taken to the bank to be paid in to the account.

Date	Client	Fee levied	Cash received	Cheques received	Transfers on account	Opening balance	Closing balance	Outstanding invoices	Due date
9/9/13	Frank T	£40.00				-£80.00	-£120.00	-£80.00	30/9/13
9/9/13	John B	£50.00	£50.00			£0.00	£0.00		
10/9/13	Bob J	£40.00		£160.00		£0.00	+£120.00		
	Steve S					-£120.00	-£120.00	-£80.00	30/9/13
10/9/13	Peter F	£40.00			£160.00	-£200.00	-£80.00	-£160.00	30/9/13
	Paula H					-£160.00	-£160.00	-£160.00	31/8/13
11/9/13	Jane Y	£50.00 -DNA			£50.00	£0.00	£0.00		
11/9/13	Sue & Jon C	£60.00	£60.00			£0.00	£0.00		
	Turnover	£280.00	Total cash	Total cheques	Total transfers		Total owed	Invoices outstanding	
		£280.00	£110.00	£160.00	£210.00		-£360.00	-£320.00	

Turnover prev. week	£3450.00
Turnover YTD	£3730.00

Banked this week	£110 + £160 = £270
Banked on date	11/9/13

103

Let's move through the example one line at a time to demonstrate how we record each client.

1. The first client on the list is "Frank T". We saw Frank this week on the 9/9/13 and, according to the contract we have with Frank, he was charged £40 for the session. Looking across columns 3, 4 & 5, we see that Frank has not made any payments this week. Instead, we see that his Closing balance (column 8) is £40 more than his Opening balance (column 7). We can also see that Frank has an outstanding invoice of £80, but that is not due until the end of the month.

2. The second client is "John B". We also saw him on the 9th, but his contract is for £50. In column 4 we see that John paid £50 in cash for this session. His opening and closing balances are the same (£0), so John owes nothing, preferring to pay-as-you-go.

3. Client 3, "Bob J", attended a session on the 10th, and his fee is £40. Interestingly, Bob chose to pay in advance, giving a cheque for £160. His opening balance was £0, but his closing balance is +£120 (the £160 cheque minus the £40 for the session). Ne the "+" against his closing balance to indicate that he has money paid in advance "on account".

4. Client 4, "Steve S", did not attend a session this week, so his opening and closing balances remain unchanged. He also has an outstanding invoice that is not due until the end of the month.

5. Then "Peter F". He attended his £40 session on the 10th, but also made an electronic transfer to pay his invoice of £160, which has been crossed out in columns 9 & 10. His Opening balance was £200 (presumably the £160 owed at the end of August, plus the previous week's £40), but his Closing balance is now £80 (the Opening Balance of £200 plus the £40 session charged on the 10th, minus the £160 transfer. £200+£40-£160=£80)

6. Client 6, "Paula H" is a concern. She has an outstanding balance of £160, and an overdue invoice of the same amount. This client appears to have ended abruptly and needs to be

chased, not only for the overdue invoice but also to re-book an appointment.

7. "Jane Y", client 7, failed to make her session on the 11th, and was charge her agreed £50 fee for not attending. She diligently made an electronic transfer of £50 that same week, meaning that her opening and closing balances were unaffected.

8. Finally, "Sue and Jon C" attended their £60 couples session and paid in cash.

Then, at the bottom of the sheet, we have some useful summaries.

- Turnover, which is the amount of money your business has "turned over", is listed for the week. It is simply all of the fees charged for all clients added up. This number is especially useful when you've been trading a while, helping you keep an eye on whether or not your business is growing or shrinking.

- Below that is a "Turnover previous week" and "Turnover year-to-date (YTD)". These track how much turnover the business is doing so far for the financial year of the company, and helps you keep track of performance.

- Then there are boxed to add-up the amount of cash and cheques received, and a corresponding area to record how much was paid into the bank that week and on what date you paid it in. This can easily be checked against your monthly bank statement (bookkeepers call this "reconciling"). The Tax Man, where he to want to look, would be especially encouraged to see that you have tracked this data as seeing it recorded in one place and replicated in another is a strong indicator that you're running your accounting system efficiently.

- Finally, there are two boxed summarising how much is owed to you (i.e. money you're going to collect from clients in the near future), and how much is owed in invoicing (i.e. money you're due to collect by the end of the that month). Keeping a close eye on this figure helps ensure that you stay on top of money owed so that it does not become out of control.

That's it. It really is that simple. Recording your takings every day, paying you're takings into your bank and summarising each week, doing your monthly invoices and checking your bank statement against what you have collected and spent *is* your accounting system. No expensive software, to mind blowing accounts training.

Invoices

Most of us will be familiar with invoices, albeit in the form of monthly household bills. The mobile phone bill, the electricity bill, the gas bill – these are all examples of invoices that we receive from suppliers of services that we pay for a month at a time.

Invoices summarise what service charges we have incurred during that period and tell us how much we owe and when we should pay that bill. It is little more than a piece of paper that has this detail summarised, and is sent to us in the post (or increasingly by email). And in your private practice, this is all it needs to be – a written summary that is sent or given to the client with the necessary details of how much is owed, when payment is required, and methods of payment.

For the initiated, creasing an invoice seems complicated, but it is not. See Appendix 2 – example invoice. Here you will see all the elements at are essential to include in any invoice:

- **An account number**: This is not strictly necessary as the "account holder" is the client. Indeed, it would be entirely reasonable to omit this detail and rely on the name and address of the client as below. However, it is good practice to create an account number rather than using the clients name, especially if you hope to get work paid for by insurance companies – it helps to protect the client identity.
- **An invoice number**: Issuing invoice numbers will help you in any communication with your clients about what

is owed. Being able to clarify that one invoice has been paid, but another is outstanding is very useful. As with account numbers above, invoice numbers are commonly required by insurance companies as they use them to keep track of what has been paid to whom.

- **The date of the invoice** to show when the invoice was created, and perhaps to state what the accounting period is that is included on this invoice.
- **The name and address of the company**, i.e. your company name and address so as to identify who the invoice is from.
- **The name and address of the client.**
- **Details of the transaction**, including dates and fees charged.
- **The total of the amount now due**.
- **Details of when the fee is due**, normally given as a specific date so as to avoid confusion.
- **Payment options** such as bank account and sort code details for electronic payment, or details of who cheques should be made out to for those who wish to pay by cheque.
- **Any other pertinent notes**, such as a reminder of late payment terms, interest charged on late payments, debt collection agency use, etc.

If you use a computerised word processor such as Microsoft Word, you can create a template invoice (copy/amend the one in appendix 2) and save it as a Template so that you can repeatedly use it for new invoices. This way, you avoid having to do everything from scratch each time you need to generate an invoice.

You could also invest in a simple accounts package that can automatically generate invoices with the client details. Packages like Sage Instant Accounts or Intuit's QuickBooks provide great functionality including the automation of invoicing and integrated mobile phone apps for visibility. However, to start with all you need is a word processor and a printer, and getting your head around this first will pay dividends later when it comes to integrating an accounting package, should you decide to do so.

Receipts and statements of account

If, as suggested, you operate a system that includes recording visits and then issuing a monthly invoice, you will be naturally creating a paper trail that you can use to prove to the Tax Man that your operations are traceable. This tractability is the central principal to any accounting system as it minimises the threat of fraud (especially in larger organisations) and, when analysed, provides a clear picture of the financial state of the business.

But invoices are not the only way of creating a paper trail. For those clients who do not choose to get a monthly invoice, it is reasonable to give them either a receipt for each payment received, or a monthly summary of payments.

The mechanics of doing statements are almost identical to the system described for invoices above – simply replace the word "Invoice" for "Statement of Account", and include an extra note to show what funds have been received and how they have been paid. See Appendix 3 for an example.

Getting underway – creating a positive cash flow

It takes courage, self-belief and a little bit of money to get you underway as a private practitioner. While we hope that reading this book will give you plenty of self-belief, the courage required – and any start up cash – will be down to you!

The problem is to do with maintaining a "positive cash flow" – a critical aspect to the success of any enterprise. The phrase simply means "having enough money in the bank to cover your bills", i.e. to be able to operate without the need for an overdraft or a loan from a bank.

Lets take a simple trade example – the baker. In order to make bread, the baker has to rent premises, install an oven, buy some tins and a mixer, and buy the ingredients. In order to do this, he needs some money – but he hasn't sold anything yet! He also needs to pay himself a "salary". So he does the following calculations based on estimated bread sales for the first month before approaching the bank for a loan.

Month 1	Transactions	Bank balance
First month's rent on the shop	- £500	- £500
Oven	- £1,000	- £1,500
Mixer	- £500	- £2,000
Tins	- £250	- £2,250
Ingredients	- £400	- £2,650
"Salary"	- £1,500	- £4,150
Anticipated bread sales – month 1	£1,200	- £2,950

At the lowest point in the month, the baker needs £4,150 in the bank to successfully operate (highlighted in yellow). So he approaches the bank and agrees an overdraft of that amount to get started.

In month two, he doubles his bread sales! He also doubles the amount of ingredients required (called variable costs in the lingo), but he now has his oven, mixer and tins, and his rent remains unchanged (called fixed costs).

Month 2	Transactions	Bank balance
Balance carried over from the previous month		- £2,950
Rent	- £500	- £3,450
Ingredients	- £800	- £4,250
"Salary"	- £1,500	- £5,750
Anticipated bread sales – month 2	£2,400	- £3,350

But spot the problem – this month he hits a low that is even lower than the month before. He goes back to the bank, has an awkward conversation with the bank manager, but manages to extend his overdraft facility believing that next month the bread sales should be double what they were in month 2.

Month 3	Transactions	Bank balance
Balance carried over from the previous month		- £3,350
Rent	- £500	- £3,850
Ingredients	- £1,600	- £5,450
"Salary"	- £1,500	- £6,950
Anticipated bread sales – month 2	£4,800	- £2,150

Once again, the baker's overdraft requires extending, but with better sales he closes the month better than the previous month. In month 4, things turn around.

Month 4	Transactions	Bank balance
Balance carried over from the previous month		- £2,150
Rent	- £500	- £2,650
Ingredients	- £1,600	- £4,250
"Salary"	- £1,500	- £5,750
Anticipated bread sales – month 2	£4,800	- £950

This example illustrates the challenge of cash flow. The reality is, of course, that bread sales are occurring throughout the month.

Summary: Your Accounting System framework

Below is an outline of set-up and on-going tasks for you to follow. This summary is designed to help you get up and running, and then remind you of the daily, weekly, monthly and annual tasks you should consider.

Setup tasks

1. Talk to a qualified accountant, tax consultant or business specialist at a bank for up-to-date advice.
2. Set up a separate bank account for the exclusive use of your practice.
3. Register your business with the Tax Man, and set up a direct debit from your practice bank account to make regular NI contributions.
4. Register yourself for the annual Self-Assessment Tax Return.
5. Create your weekly Takings Journal (see Appendix 1).
6. Develop blank Invoice (Appendix 2) and Statement of Account (Appendix 3) forms (known as "Templates" in Microsoft Office Word).
7. Pay your business (Bob) a "loan", arrange an over draft or a bank loan to get you started.
8. Sort out your credit card processing facility.
9. Open for business!

Daily tasks

- Take any cash money from clients and store it securely.
- Record all transactions in your Takings Journal.

Weekly tasks

- Go to the bank and pay in cash and cheques.
- Summarise your weeks takings in the Takings Journal.
- Check your bank statement to see if any of your clients have paid you directly into your bank account (e.g. paying their invoices)
- Summarise balances for individual clients and record the "closing balance" for each client.
- Carry forward the "closing balance" from this week into next weeks "opening balance" for each client in readiness for next weeks trading.

Monthly tasks

- Issue invoices to customers that you have agreed to work with in this way.
- Chase invoices (and if necessary issue reminders/penalties) that are over due.
- Issue "statement of account" summaries to all other customers.
- Check your bank statement for income and expenditure transactions.
- Add up your expenditure for the month and estimate what it is going to cost you (rent, memberships, continued education etc.) for next month. Set that money aside so that you have it in the bank to cover your bills for the coming month (see notes on cash-flow above)
- Pay yourself a "salary" by transferring what you can afford into your personal bank account. Remember to keep some aside (we suggest 25-30%) for personal income tax and National Insurance.

Annual tasks

- Do your tax return (payments due by January 31st, but you can do the return anytime for the previous year)
- Review the performance of your business and set financial objectives that might include future investment in advertising (e.g. Google AdWords) or training.

Get additional advise

The model we have explained above is based on our experience of setting up in private practice, honed through experiences of getting things wrong! The model is based around the "Sole Trader" approach, which has benefits and drawbacks like any system. In our experience, this approach, backed up by a good level of professional insurance, is simple and adequate for the profession. However, we are not qualified accountants or tax consultants, so we would recommend that you get additional advice from a tax or accounting professional, or from a business specialist at a bank.

Section 4 – Practice management systems

By now, we hope that you have a good understanding of the basics of marketing, have identified a niche, have a website up and running, and have enough understanding of the finance and accounting requirements to get you underway. That leaves the small matter of actually getting going!

In this section, we aim to do three things:

A. To walk you through the practicalities of getting a practice up and running, covering things like what to look for as you search for premises, an indication of the costs involved in setting up, and a rough idea of how quickly you might be able to earn money.

B. To cover the day-to-day aspects of running a practice, such as keeping records, tailoring contracts and how best to be contactable by your clients, and the development of "good practice".

C. To inspire you to make your practice and an excellent practice, monitoring quality and performance so that you can get better and grow in confidence *and* earnings.

Part A – Growing your practice from scratch

Finding premises

Finding premises is actually quite difficult. There are many properties available, but finding a location that is suitable, and a space that is fit for purpose is hard work. Many counsellors opt to operate from their own homes, but that too has some restrictions that need to be carefully considered.

The key factor in your decision-making must continue to be your intended clients. You should keep them front of mind while you make your choices.

Take transportation links, for example. Ease of access and security must all be carefully considered, and the best location for your practice room is <u>a space that works best for your target market</u>. This means really thinking about who they are, what they will be familiar with, what they will be comfortable with, and how they will get to you. There is no point having a counselling service for the elderly that requires them to walk half-a-mile up an inclined driveway. Or having a counselling service for eating disorders above a bakers!

If your target market are likely to drive themselves to your location (i.e. you expect the majority of your target market to have their own cars and be confident in using them) then the location should probably be governed by whether it is close enough to major transportation hubs (motorways, dual carriageways, 'A' roads etc., or better still at popular cross road locations where people can get to you from a variety of directions), if the location is easy to find and if there is easy parking near by or on-site. If, on the other hand, your target market is not so mobile, then perhaps a town centre location served by regular bus connections is the best place to base yourself.

Perhaps your target market will be really sensitive to being seen by others waiting around for their appointment or entering a building with a big sign over the door "Counselling 4 U" – again, town centre locations provide easy excuses for people to be seen without raising suspicions, and anonymous buildings or multi-purpose buildings make it easy for sensitive clients to blend into the background.

The sorts of premises you might consider include:

- **Working from home** in a spare room (see below for more).
- **Office space**. There are thousands of empty offices around the country, but they present the private practitioner with a number of challenges. To get a space in an office building, you will typically need to sign up to an agreed lease period (measured in years, not months!), kit the room out, pay rates and basic

maintenance. And offices are normally designed to accommodate 5 to 500 employees, but you just need just 1 small room. Consequently, it is almost impossible to find suitable office premises on your own - clubbing together with other counsellors and renting an office between you and sharing the costs will make this option more feasible.

- **Serviced offices** offer considerably more flexible hire terms, but they are more expensive than leased offices. Serviced offices typically offer extras as part of a package deal – telephone, internet, receptionists and reception space, and other administrative resources like printers and photocopiers. You'll need to consider privacy for your clients with this option, especially when clients are moving about corridors and more public reception spaces, but the simplicity of this solution does make it worth considering.

- There are a good number of **dedicated practice rooms** available for hire by the hour or day or part there-of, and these represent an excellent first starting place for the new practitioner. Take a look in the back of a BACP journal for many examples. These are great because they are designed for purpose, are typically low risk in not requiring much of a long-term commitment, and can often be cancelled at short notice. This pay-as-you-go type scheme is especially useful for the new therapist, paying by the hour or block of hours and off-setting that cost against the client fee that you're able to charge. However, this option does become too expensive once the economies of scale make your own office financially viable.

- Under-utilised **treatment rooms** in hair dressers, dentists, doctors surgeries, etc., spare rooms above high-street shops, or in local community centres are another useful source of space. And often the owners are not even aware that they could be being used by therapists like yourself. But be driven by where you think your target clients are going to be comfortable, and then look in those areas for options that might suit.

At all times, your clients need to be front-of-mind, so imagine yourself as a client entering these spaces.

Working from home

Many counsellors choose to work from home, converting a front room, a summer house, a garage or spare bedroom into a practice room. Let's go over some of the pro's and con's of this approach:

Pro's

- The obvious benefit of working from home is that you do not have to pay for a separate office. Indeed, you can justifiably charge your company ("Bob" introduced in Section 3) a "rent" to cover the use of a room, and a contribution towards your utilities bills etc. (but check how much with an accountant – it has to be a fair proportion, not your total bill!)
- You do not have far to travel to your office!
- You get to control the environment.
- Anonymous residential space is not likely to cause embarrassment to clients sensitive to being seen by people they know.

Con's

- Is your place easy to find, and does it offer somewhere easy / free to park?
- Your clients will know where you live! Your personality and family life and wealth status and tastes will all inevitably be imprinted on the therapy. Your clients will make a large number of presumptions about you and

your life that risk, if not very carefully thought through, invading the therapeutic space.

- You are responsible for maintaining a safe access for your client to be on your property – liability insurance is an absolute must, as well as being sure to maintain the approach to your door in the middle of winter, and that rug in the hallway.
- Will you have to modify your property for wheelchair access (if that is a client group you envisage working with)?
- Will you have to walk clients through your living room to get to your therapy room? Who else will be there? What else might your clients get to know about you as they walk through? How tidy will your house need to be kept in order to make these spaces unobtrusive? And what about providing toilet facilities?
- What will your neighbours think?! This is a serious concern to some neighbourhoods as, technically, you might not be able to run a business from home. You should always check with your local council to see if you need any specific permissions.
- If you have children, how good are they going to be at not disturbing you while you're in-session?
- If you have pets, how would you deal with a client who has an allergy to cats or a fear of dogs?
- You know your house, and you probably feel secure there – but is this an assumption that your clients might not share?
- It can be difficult to "leave work" when you work from home – working from a separate office enables you to leave work at work, and go home and relax, with the two distinct locations helping you to separate your home life from your work life.

I would like to share an anecdote with you from my own personal experience. My first introduction to counselling was as a client in my early 30's. My counsellor, a middle-aged lady, ran her practice from a converted spare bedroom in her home. The route to her practice room was through the front door, along the corridor, through the kitchen, up the stairs and back round on myself to enter the therapy room. She was very good at maintaining this space – the kitchen was always tidy, I never met anyone else in the house on this journey, and as it was my first time in therapy I knew no different, so it didn't seem too strange to me.

But this journey through the house meant that I gleaned certain details about my therapist – the photo's of children on a wall were, I presumed, of her children. A mention of a husband. A cat curled up by a radiator. Clients, I discovered, are keen to know that therapists are "real" – it reassures them. And they typically have never heard of projection or transference!

One day something unusual happened. En route to the therapy room, at the top of the stairs before turning back on myself to the therapy room, in full view was her bedroom – she had inadvertently left the door open, and I could see directly into what for many is the most intimate space in our homes. Mercifully, her smalls were not lying on the floor, and her negligée was not hanging up on the end of the bed! Nonetheless, she was embarrassed, apologised and quickly closed the door. Thankfully, her experience as a therapist meant that she was able to handle it well, integrating the experience into the therapy.

This anecdote serves to demonstrate what is important of any environment – it is inevitable that your choice of office space will carry some aspects of you, everything from the choice of artwork on the wall to the furniture or the books on your bookshelf. Even if you choose to have nothing on the walls and not a book in sight, you will be projecting a message with that decision. Far better, then, to develop the capacity to *integrate* these factors into your practice, using anything that is presented as an opportunity to make a therapeutic intervention. "Familiarity breed's contempt", so the saying goes – the assumptions that we make about a space that *we* are familiar with can breed a complacency that means we might not think to carefully consider our clients experience of our space.

You will need to balance your personal safety, the therapeutic "efficiency" of the space, it's convenience and its cost in any choice you make about premises. Be guided by what works best for your target market – put yourself in their shoes – and then factor in the other aspects of cost and safety in order to arrive at a shortlist of locations and property types. Then use the internet, or simply walk around your target area to find possible locations.

Set-up costs

Any new business venture typically needs some financial injection to get it going. Indeed, you have probably already invested a good deal of time and money into becoming trained as a therapist, and getting a practice off the ground is no different. From our own experience, these are the sorts of costs that you are likely to need to accommodate before you begin to get paying clients.

Many counsellors allow practices to grow "organically", perhaps not needing a second income or having other paid employment on a part-time basis until there is enough business flowing. But we would encourage you to take a more business-like attitude towards creating a successful practice, with targets or a budget plan to try and attain, otherwise the risk is that your practice will never really take off.

We have split the estimates below into categories of organic, moderate and aggressive strategies depending on how rapidly you intend to grow your practice. Of course, the reality is that you're more likely to start at the "organic" category and move up towards a more intensive strategy as your practice (and confidence) builds.

Websites

Organic: Build your own website using Internet providers. £25 plus £5 a month.

Moderate: Use a specialist template based service provider - £250 set-up costs, plus £15 a month.

Aggressive: Professionally developed website. £500-£1000. Consider having additional websites to offer services to other similar niches.

Search Engine Optimisation

Organic: Leave search engines to find you - £0

Moderate: Use a computer based SEO technique. £50

Aggressive: Employ the services of a professional to manage your SEO - £250/month.

AdWords

Organic: Don't spend anything on advertising – simply wait for clients to find your website Network with other counsellors and ask them to recommend you or pass on clients they are unable to accommodate.

Moderate: £50 a month for 3 months to get you underway, then only use it to grow in bursts. Bid rates set at recommended level. Network with other counsellors and ask them to recommend you or pass on clients they are unable to accommodate.

Aggressive: £150 a month for 6 months. Bid rate set high to ensure that your ads are on page 1. Network with other counsellors and ask them to recommend you or pass on clients they are unable to accommodate. Approach insurance companies and health-care providers and ask them to send you clients.

Premises

Organic: Pay-as-you-go room rental, or work from a spare room at home.

Moderate: Look to share a room with a few other counsellors or rent pay-as-you-go dedicated practice rooms.

Aggressive: Serviced office space or dedicated practice rooms.

Diary

Organic: Paper diary from a stationary shop. £10.

Moderate: Smartphone on a monthly contract. £25 a month.

Aggressive: Smartphone on a monthly contract. £25 a month, plus an online calendar for people to book slots themselves via the internet.

Payment facilities

Organic: None – stick to cash and cheque, and give out a bank account number/sort code for those who want to transfer money to you electronically.

Moderate: Use a smartphone based card reader linked to an iPhone or similar. £100 set up cost + transaction fee.

Aggressive: Bank issued card reader. £varies

Literature

Organic: Nothing – invest in this later.

Moderate: Business cards and leaflets.

Aggressive: Business cards and leaflets. Post leaflets to local GPs, and ask for bundles to be left in strategic places. Posters on A boards in the town centre, and a range of helpful subject-specific leaflets.

Making realistic projections about income

It is exciting to play with a calculator and work out how much you might earn from counselling. 10 clients a week at £45 a client is £450 a week. Multiply that by 52 weeks a year and that's a potential income of £23,400 (£1,950 a month). 15 clients a week at £50 a client is £750 a week. Multiply that by 52 weeks a year and that's a potential income of £39,000 (£3,250 a month before tax).

Exciting indeed. But is it realistic? There are some important considerations that need to be made when arriving at a realistic projection about income.

First of all, do not forget your fixed costs. Room rental, insurances, website costs, advertising costs, supervision costs, membership, telephone and Internet charges, and CPD costs – you will typically have to pay these regardless of how many clients you see.

Secondly, don't forget to factor in holidays for yourself – if you're on holiday, you won't be seeing clients, so you won't be earning money. As a rule of thumb, multiply your weekly expectations by 48 weeks in a year, and give yourself 4 weeks (52-48=4) off a year. (This also makes it easy to calculate monthly incomes – multiply the weekly income by 4 weeks and you'll have a rough idea of monthly income (4x12=48).

An approximate rule-of-thumb is to factor in a 10% variance to your weekly projections. This means that if, say, you work out that you need £600 per week before fixed costs, factor in 10% of £600 = £60 per week to be put aside every week to cover holidays. This would mean that you would then need £660 a week, leaving £60 in the business to accumulate to cover 4 weeks holiday a year.

Thirdly, don't forget that your clients will not necessarily take holidays at the same time as you! The impact of this is felt especially during school term breaks, Christmas and the six-week of summer – factor this into your projections, and we would estimate that this would account for an additional 5% variance.

Fourthly, don't underestimate the impact of the weather. Even if you work from home, your clients will need to be able to get to you. Snow is guaranteed to cause disruption, and high winds can also be problematic.

Fifth, short notice cancellations are inevitable for individuals that lead busy lives and/or have children that require looking after. Most counsellors will operate a system whereby they will charge for clients who cancel at short notice (typically 24hrs), but you will need to decide how you implement this. Perhaps rather than rigidly enforcing such a policy, you may decide to enforce this for "repeat offenders" (I run a 3-strikes-and-you're-out-rule) rather than those who occasionally find themselves having to shoot off and pick up a sick child from school. Either way, you will need to consider how this might impact your regular income.

Sixth, think about how shift workers or those that wish to have fortnightly rather than weekly sessions might impact your weekly calculations.

Finally, don't forget to factor in a tax provision as previously discussed.

By the time this has all happened, those early calculations are pretty inaccurate. Once you've added it all up, we would recommend that you work on a variance of 20%, systematically putting this amount aside to accommodate fluctuations in income. Therefore, to achieve a reliable £600 clear income per week, put aside 20% = £120 every week – that's £720 a week to earn, not £600. Working in this way may seem impossible, especially at first when you're just getting going, but as soon as you are able you should seek put this sort of a proportion aside to help you avoid getting to the end of a month and hot having anything left in the pot with which to pay yourself.

Costs	Per annum	Per month	Per week (48 week year)
Room rental	£4,200	**£350**	£87.50
Supervision	£1,200	**£100**	£25.00
Liability insurance	**£150**	£38	£3.13
BACP membership	**£150**	£38	£3.13
Website costs	£180	**£15**	£3.75
Advertising	£600	**£50**	£12.50
CPD	**£150**	£38	£3.13
Mobile phone	£300	**£25**	£6.25
Internet	£180	**£15**	£3.75
TOTALs	£7,110	£668	£148.13

Income target/objective	Per annum	Per month	Per week (48 week year)
"Take home"		£2,000	
Provision for NI & Tax (approx. 1/3rd of income)		£1,000	
Target income before tax and costs	£36,000	£3,000	
Plus 20% variance provision of target income		£600	
Plus costs (above)		£668	
Total income from clients		£4,268	£1,066.88

Number of clients at £40 per client	107	26.7
Or		
Number of clients at £50 per client	85	21.3

The above example starts by forecasting the likely costs. Some are monthly, some annually (shown in bold font), but the table shows the cost as annual, monthly and weekly provisions. In this example, you can see that you need to earn £148 a week just to operate.

Next the calculation looks at income, and specifies a desired or target "take home" (i.e. after tax) income. This is the amount of money you would like to have in your bank account after tax, £2000 per month in this example.

Then we put aside an amount to pay that pesky tax bill (see "Tax" in Section 3 - Accounting Basics) to arrive at an income before costs have been calculated, in this case £3000 per month.

Then we add on the suggested 20% variance to cover holidays, absences etc. as detail above. This adds on another £600 to the target income.

Then add costs (£668 per month) and we arrive at £4268 per month (£1066.88 per week) as a target to collect and back from clients.

If you charge £40 per client, then you'll need to do 26.7 (rounded up to 27) clients per week on average for 48 weeks per year. If you charge £50 per client, then you'll need to do 21.3 (rounded to 21) clients per week on average for 48 weeks per year.

This client number is a target. Remember that you have put in a provision to the calculations, meaning that you have a cushion in place. The calculations air on the side of caution, reducing risk and being conservative in approach – personally, I would rather be able to sleep well at night knowing that I can afford to pay the mortgage each month, and have some in reserve for a sudden drop in client numbers because the weather closes in or because half my clients go away on holiday in August.

Be your own Sales Manager

Sales Managers in any business are responsible for turning enquiries into customers, diligently ensuring that enquiries are followed up promptly and professionally. They have targets, are profit driven and are part of a broader sales and marketing team, feeding-back information to their marketing colleagues about what is working and what is not in order to drive up sales.

This is an uncomfortable role for many people, especially those with character types that make them naturally suited to caring professions like counselling. The role brings up anxieties about being pushy, persuasive, coercive, or even down right misleading, emulating the proverbial "used-car salesman", or using manipulative techniques to prey on other peoples fears and anxieties to sell them something they just don't need.

Clearly, such an aggressive approach in counselling would be both unethical and inappropriate. Yet in order to create a successful private practice, you will still need to have the ability to "sell" your services, and as we have seen above, we will need to achieve a target in order to achieve an income.

Discomfort about this role might mean that when enquiries do come through, counsellors come across as lacking in confidence. The danger here is that this lack of confidence as a "sales manager" might be projected as a lack of confidence as a counsellor, the potential client perceiving the counsellor as un-containing just at that critical moment of vulnerability as the client has taken the unprecedented step of phoning you to make an appointment.

Sales Managers understand and are confident about the "product", in this case the ability to successfully contain the client and work with their problems. Creating trust as a Sales Manager means maintaining a clear, perhaps even frank reality about the capability of the "product", and not overselling or overstating what it can do. This moment is you and your clients' first step towards a working alliance where they develop trust in your ability to help them help themselves.

The marketing techniques we have outlined are designed to simply make you easy to find, allowing potential clients to find you and contact you by phone or by email in their own time. The information you put on your website should, if correctly done, "sell" your "product" by being clear without being misleading, by being informative without being coercive. This means that you do need to be on the phone chasing prospects. Instead, you simply need to develop the necessary competence to convert enquiries into clients.

The key to success in this role is to understand that the potential client has already taken a truly monumental step by simply contacting you. When I review the statistics from my website, I see that there are far more people browsing than there are enquiries made. This is to be expected – potential clients are searching, struggling with their own capacity to cope, fighting with themselves about when and if to ask for help, and terrified about what they might discover about themselves – in order to make that call or send that email they have read and re-read the information on my website, dug deep and found the courage necessary to ask for help. Therefore, the Sales Managers' job is not to persuade, rather to provide some simple, humane reassurance that you are not going to perform a frontal lobotomy or call the men in white coats! You just need to be yourself and make the necessary arrangements for this terrified and troubled individual to take that all-important first step.

At this point, the counselling relationship has already started. In fact, it started when they first began to read your website material. So extend the same principals of confidentiality and sensitivity as you would a client visiting your offices. This might mean asking them to hold on while you go into a separate room to take their call (thereby letting them know that you're sensitive to confidentiality). It might mean checking with them that they are ok to talk if you have called them back. It might mean leaving your name and number, but not your "counsellor" title on an answer phone message in case someone else has access to those messages.

Tools for the job

A diary is an absolute must for any private practitioner. Paper diaries are the simplest (and help to form a "paper trail" of evidence that the Tax Man likes to see), but electronic diaries like those available on smart phones are handy and easy to see.

If you choose to use a paper diary, can you be confident in your ability to not loose it? And if you did loose it, would it risk exposing your clients' confidentiality? Equally, if you choose an electronic diary, is it reliable?

Personally, I prefer a smart phone that combines phone, text messaging, email, contacts and a diary. It lives in my pocket, and means I am never far from being able to see incoming messages and never risk loosing my diary – a device like Apple's iPhone can be set to automatically back everything up to a website (iCloud via an Apple ID account), so if the worse was to happen and the device was lost or stolen, then you always have an accurate copy online. Such devices also require you to enter a PIN code to unlock the device, making them secure even if they are lost or stolen. And iPhone's even have a tracking system to help you find it if you misplace it. Don't forget that such a device can justifiably be seen as a business tool, so "Bob" can pay for it.

You may even consider going one better and getting either a tablet (e.g. iPad) or a laptop computer. Such devices are less portable than a smart phone, but the more computerised you go, the more automated your systems can be, helping you track clients, send them invoices / statements of account, and keep accurate diaries. There is an increasing array of software designed to help small business owners, but take care to get what you actually need rather than being persuaded to buy software that may (at least at first) be an unnecessarily over-complicated hammer to crack what might be a simple nut.

A computer and a printer are useful tools, especially for printing and/or emailing invoices to clients. For best results, choose a simple laser type printer (e.g. HP LaserJet 1102) rather than an inkjet or bubble jet type – while the printer itself will cost a little more, the finish is better and the ink cartridge will last longer saving you money in the long run.

A cash box is also a good idea, helping you keep your takings safe and in one place. And a filing cabinet with a lock and suitable dividers also helps with security, keeping records locked away safely.

Finally, think about your own comfort. I spend many hours in my practice room, so a heater, soft lighting and a really, really good chair are essential.

Part B – Developing good practice

Now we move on to consider the day-to-day aspects of running a practice, such as keeping records, tailoring contracts, and the development of "good practice". Chief among these is the critical need for good supervision.

<u>The importance of good supervision</u>

Merely ticking the box of satisfying your professional obligations in having the minimum amount of supervision required is nether adequate nor in the spirit of acting professionally as a therapist. We cannot stress enough the importance of having good supervision. By this we mean having access to a good supervisor, AND developing a good, open, frank relationship with that supervisor. One without the other is a recipe for disaster, and in private practice, a disaster is absolutely to be avoided.

Theoretically, anyone who is qualified as a supervisor should be good enough. Arguably, however, the private practitioner really benefits from supervision conducted by someone who is experience in private practice themselves – their hard-won knowledge of what works and what does not is invaluable to the new private practitioner, supporting you clinically and offering practical guidance on running your practice based on their own experience.

But the biggest element of a successful relationship with a supervisor is your capacity to be absolutely candid with him or her. You need to be able to talk about your cock-ups, the school-boy errors, the clumsy interventions, the lost-ness you feel with certain clients, and the way in which you feel overwhelmed by others. You need to be able to say how you fancy this client, or feel sexually intimidated by that client. You need to develop this level of candidness not because it fulfils some twisted sadomasochistic game play, but because it is safe. Nothing hidden means nothing to hide. It allows the rawness of projection and transference to be brought into the room with the supervisor, and goes a long way towards ensuring that risks do not build up in your practice.

Ask yourself why you bring certain types of clients to supervision and not others? Do you bring lots of new clients to supervision – perhaps this reflects your own anxiety about taking on new clients? Do you feel ambivalent towards supervision – perhaps this reflects tiredness in you? Do you feel anger towards your supervisor – perhaps this reflects a feeling of vulnerability or of being unsupported? Do you only bring the "good" cases to supervision – perhaps you do this because you're in need of encouragement – or perhaps you're scared of being criticised or feeling inadequate or intimidated by a supervisor in whom you are in awe?!

Like any healthy relationship, the relationship you have with your supervisor ought to be open, full of honest communication, supportive, nurturing, and open to feedback and constructive criticism. You might also consider having more than one supervisor, splitting your client work between them. Doing this may not seem logical, but it halves the risk of a poor relationship hiding certain clients from your supervisor and leaving you exposed.

We would suggest that good practice is to adopt a systematic approach to client supervision, bringing each and every one of your clients to supervision in turn. Try placing your clients on a rota, going through them all one by one, thereby preventing any unconscious selection or de-selection. In <u>Part C – Monitoring and boosting performance</u>, and in <u>Appendix 4</u>, we will introduce a client tracking form that includes a means of monitoring when this client was last included in supervision.

If that is not practical, at least try and be aware of any tendency to "cherry pick" clients to bring to supervision, or to avoid bringing a client to supervision. If you find yourself falling foul to either of these tendencies, your internal supervisor should be quick to acknowledge this and do something about it!

There is a school of thought that, rather than going through clients systematically, allowing unconscious selection / de-selection is useful in exposing those hard-to-spot transferences. Asking yourself why you're presenting a particular client to supervision is as revealing as asking a client why they are looking for counselling now and why they selected you amongst the many other counsellors out there.

However, it is the clients that you do not bring that are the ones most likely to trip you up – be careful to develop your own internal supervisor, a skill that is helped greatly by the level of candidness you can develop with your actual supervisor. It takes time to develop the skill of being aware that you "hate" this client, are "repulsed" by that client, or feel the urge to hug one client or feel sexually attracted to another, and further time to develop the skill to integrate that knowledge into the therapy live in the room with a client. Utilise supervision to develop this skill, and in so doing is a great way of keeping the relationship with you clients therapeutic regardless of whether your feelings for them are hate, love, lust, repulsion, frustration, boredom, or indifference.

Record keeping

The BACP is clear on the need to protect the identity of your clients. Practically, this means two things:

1. Keep contact details and invoicing / accounts on one system
2. Keep session notes on a separate, anonymized (i.e. no names on your notes) system that does not directly identify your clients (maybe it has a client code or initials)

Golden rule: keep both systems physically separate from one another.

The security of records is paramount. The nightmare scenario is loosing your notebook somewhere between your office and the coffee shop. We would strongly recommend the following:

- Wherever possible, use password protected electronic record keeping with a robust electronic backup system.
  - This is especially useful for contact and accounts information.
  - A smartphone like an iPhone will enable you to password protect your phone, your online account and any associated computers.
  - Keep your personal life and professional life separate. Be sure to know which of your contacts is a client, and which is a friend/family member. If you're going to struggle with this, use entirely different devices. (This has the added benefit of being able to turn your "work" phone off completely at the end of the day).
- If you must use paper:
  - Use individual sheets of paper and store them in a "client folder" (you can also include tracking sheets in this folder such as those suggested in Appendix 4). This is preferable to a notebook that is easier to loose.
  - Do not take your notes out of your practice room. Notes get lost when they are transported. If at all possible, have a lockable filing cabinet in your practice room, and leave them there.

    o If you are unable to have a lockable filing cabinet in your room, use a lockable, portable storage unit like a "pilots case".

The taking of notes seems to be an issue of personal preference amongst the therapists we know. Here are some of the methods and pro's/con's to these methods:

- Take notes on paper *during a session*: useful for capturing little details, but can cause anxiety in the mind of the client that you're writing something they cannot see!
- Take no notes at all, preferring instead to rely on what the brain recalls: useful for security (!), terrible for those of use with poor memories! The more humanistic practitioners tend to feel that this is the best as it allows them to be completely present in the room, and rely instead on what floats to the top of their minds to determine what is significant.
- Summarise sessions by writing a short paragraph or two at the end of each session. This is the preferred system, and is easy to do electronically, helping you avoid paper. And if you tie this in with a good client tracking record (see Appendix 4), then it can be a useful means by which you get an overview of your client.

Mobiles, hyper-availability and Social Media

Our experience of counsellors in training covered some of the basics of looking after yourself, but we wanted to write a short section to give you some practical tips on other areas to aid self-care.

The first of these is the issue of mobile phones. Messages, emails, texts, and the immediacy of a very personal mobile device has created an impression of hyper-availability. Good practice for counsellors is to (a) have a separate "work" mobile, and (b) to turn it off once your working day is complete. It also pays dividends in the long run to be slow at replying to text messages so as to not create an impression that you're available at the whim of the client.

The nightmare scenario is getting a text that wakes you up at 3am to read that one of your more vulnerable clients is intending to commit suicide. Or they send message after message, phone call after phone call in an attempt to get hold of you. While these symptoms are significant, and important to the counselling room, failure to control your availability risks inviting clients to abuse the boundaries of the counselling contract. And if they are struggling at 3am, they need to use NHS services, not you.

In a similar vein, you need to be especially careful about your use of and availability via social media channels. Twitter, FaceBook, Instagram etc. have become so ubiquitous that we can unwittingly find that what we thought was our private life is viewable by our clients. We would recommend being very, very hard to find!

Misspell your profile name or use a nickname, have a profile picture that is not identifiable, turn your security settings up to maximum to make it as hard as possible for clients to search for you. And believe me, there is a proportion of clients who will do exactly that.

Professional Wills

Just recently, we lost a dear friend and counsellor following complications after surgery. She had helped a great number of clients over the many years of her practice, and still had a considerable number of clients that were "on her books", let alone those many clients to whom she was only a phone call away from doing some more work at some point in the future.

The sudden nature of her death meant that clients began turning up for their appointments as arranged the week after what was supposed to be routine surgery. Sadly, this meant that there was a steady stream of clients knocking at her door (she worked from home) to be met by a grieving husband left to explain that their counsellor had died.

As sad as this was for him having to re-tell the news over and over, it was also devastating for her clients. Endings are complicated enough for clients!

As morbid as this might be, it is a reminder of how important it is for some arrangements to be put in place for these circumstances within your own practice. It is not enough to assume that your supervisor is the person to whom this responsibility should fall – it is your responsibility to ensure that adequate provision is made for the sake of your clients.

These "professional wills" are meant to accommodate your instructions should the worst happen for you. You should:

- Keep a record of current clients (perhaps in conjunction with your diary) so that your nominated "executor" would be able to make contact with all your clients in advance of them turning up to an empty chair.
- Ensure that your notes are up-to-date and, without compromising security, should be available to your nominated executor.

- Make explicit arrangements with your next of kin to ensure that the agreement you have in place with your executor is understood.
- Make explicit arrangements with a trusted and skilled professional colleague to be your executor. This might include a financial provision within your will to ensure this individual is not out-of-pocket should the worse happen.

Part C – Monitoring and boosting performance

All good businesses monitor a range of "key performance indicators" (KPIs) that together give an indication about the performance of the business. Some of these measures are hard data – things like profit, the number of customers, the return rate of faulty product, market share, price comparisons and costs of raw materials.

Some measures are more subjective, relying on an aggregated collection of opinions to form an overall impression. To do this, businesses invite customers to provide feedback, offer loyalty schemes and survey the perceptions of brands.

The effectiveness of employees is also measured. Production rates, manufacturing errors, sales effectiveness, complaints and customer satisfaction feedback.

These KPIs form a "dashboard" of information, all of which is collected and poured over by the leaders of the business. Like the dashboard in your car that shows the status of the vehicle, and flashes red when something is going wrong, so KPIs provide an indication of the status of a business, and help business leaders to see ways of improving efficiency, boosting sales, exploring new market opportunities and developing customer loyalty.

But what is good performance in counselling and how and why do we measure that performance? After all, a private practice is hardly an international brand. Yet measuring the performance of your business and the performance of you as a therapist reflects a professional attitude that is fitting to the profession.

Monitoring the performance of your practice is not just about your capacity to grow the business and make money from doing so, but also for ensuring that the work you start with your clients is work that you can afford to continue with them. At the same time, monitoring the performance of you as a therapist is a way of ensuring that you are doing the very best job for your clients as possible, providing them with a service that is focused on expediently bringing positive benefit to their lives.

Measurement and a culture of feedback – white coats and people pleasers

Arguably, failing to monitor the effectiveness of you as a therapist is tantamount to misconduct. Let's consider it from the point of view of you as a patient - if you went to GP and you found out that they got their diagnosis correct 60% of the time, would you care? Of course you would – it might mean that you were one of the 40% whose diagnosis was missed! The consequences are too much to comprehend.

But most of the time we as patients assume that our GP is knowledgeable, diligent and well trained, monitored and accountable. It doesn't really occur to most of us that this highly trained professional would do anything other than conduct themselves with utmost professionalism and strive to make the right diagnosis every time.

While this attitude of unquestioned authority towards such professionals is changing (we are increasingly being encouraged to seek other medical opinions within the NHS), when we see someone in a "white coat" of a profession we typically presume that this person has the knowledge and authority. We respect their opinion and we do not question it.

But here's the scary thing – our clients think of us in the same way. They presume that we know what we're talking about. They presume that we represent a level of professionalism that would be no different if they were sitting in front of another therapist in the next street. They presume that we have the answers, some mystical wisdom that could change their lives (and if you think this is true, you're in the wrong profession!) Most clients will not have previous experience of counselling, so you're it – you represent the whole of the counselling profession for your clients.

Today, the profession of counselling is still largely unregulated. Is the training from this adult education centre the same as from that university? Is an accredited counsellor any more or less effective and professional than a non-accredited one? Is a BACP member therapist better or worse than a UKCP member therapist? Is one therapist more effective than another?

If you work for an agency, then monitoring is probably already underway. Agencies, especially those that receive external funding, are typically required to demonstrate to committee members that they are delivering what they said they would in order to win the funding that they receive. Similarly, if you were to take work from an insurance company, they would typically want to know that you are measurably helping clients to overcome, say, a driving phobia or a crash trauma, and they would look for written evidence.

Various attempts have been made over the years to develop mechanisms for tracking the effectiveness of therapy. Perhaps best known is CORE (http://www.coreims.co.uk) which is a before, during and after questionnaire designed to assess the level of improvement felt by clients. Similarly, there is the Impact of Events Scale (Creamer, Bell & Failla (2003)) for measuring the progress of therapy at overcoming a traumatic event.

But what if you're not required to produce a report. Can we put client complaints down to "their stuff", a transference or a projection of anger being exhibited in the therapy. Sure, it is entirely possible that clients *are* expressing their emotions and misplacing them in the therapy room, but is it also entirely possible that they're angry or frustrated because the therapy just isn't working for them, that they feel vulnerable or unsupported, that you're crap?! The only way that you're going to know is to put the client at the very heart of the therapy, and that means being a professional about wanting real feedback.

Lets illustrate this with an example from personal relationships. I am a stocky, ex-rugby playing 100kg man who is capable of throwing his weight around. By contrast, my wife is a good 6 inches shorter than me, and half my weight. The risk to our relationship is that I could unwittingly dominate – in arguments especially, I could unintentionally impose my physicality and watch arguments deteriorate into a demonstration of who has the largest lungs and the loudest voice, and I would probably win this every time simply because of genetics. Being conscious of this, I make a very special effort to reduce my physical profile when we argue, and I pay particular attention to seeking to ensure that my wife has the opportunity to express herself, bending over backwards to create an *environment of safety* for her to say-it-how-she-sees-it, and deliberately soliciting feedback from her to underline to her that her opinion matters to me.

It should be no different for our clients. While you might never have played rugby, you are nonetheless in a position of authority in the counselling room, and so your clients should be encouraged to express honest feedback, to be made to *feel safe to tell you about the therapy,* that it isn't working for them, or that they are struggling with the material, that they find you or the environment intimidating. This is especially difficult for those people pleaser clients who want to be a "good client" – they don't want to admit that they don't get it, or that your interventions cut a bit too deep, or that they feel stupid because they just didn't see what was happening in their lives. It is, therefore, your professional duty to create an *environment of safety* where your clients are encouraged to feedback to you, helping to underline that such feedback is a welcomed part of the process, that they feel valued by you as part of a collaborative effort towards their health and the development of you as a therapist.

One of the leading lights in this area is Scott D Miller who has developed a complete system called Feedback Informed Treatment (FIT) (http://scottdmiller.com) including training and forms for feedback/measurement. But whether or not you get into form filling, *it is the humble attitude of equality and open client feedback that is at the heart of successfully growing your practice professionally.*

How might this be done? Actually, with this humble attitude in your heart, it is surprisingly easy to find the right empathic language and phrases to openly encourage your client to feedback. Try some of these:

- *"I wonder how you're finding our sessions?"*
- *"It really helps me improve how I can help my clients by asking them for their feedback – I wonder if you can tell me what you like and what you dislike about my approach?"*
- *"I can see that some of the material we're delving into is hard work for you – do you think we're going at a pace that is working for you?"*
- *"Sometimes therapy can feel like a bit of a long slog, no? How are you finding it?"*

KPIs in Counselling

Performance in any business is typically summarised through the measurement of a list of key indicators, and your practice is no different. Good therapists will develop an intuitive sense of this with their clients, but for the rest of us, or for practices that are busy, a more mechanical, deliberate system helps to ensure that signs are not overlooked. The list below is not exhaustive, but suitable KPIs for your private practice might include:

- The "did not attend" rate (DNA rate) – a client who begins to DNA might be a client who is struggling with you and/or the therapy. Perhaps they are struggling with the material? Perhaps they are finding your interventions too strong or not strong enough, or perhaps the therapy isn't yielding the improvement they were hoping for, and so they DNA as a sort of passive-aggressive protest to slowly separate themselves from you the therapist.

- Time keeping – in a similar way, clients who are perpetually early, late, bang-on time or clients that can't wait to get out of the door or, conversely, push the session by revealing delicate subject matter towards the end of the session are all communicating something important about the therapy. Changes in this behaviour are indicative of changes in the therapy for the client. Recording this information will help you to track any changes in this sort of client behaviour.

- Engagement – is the client staying-on or straying-from the subject matter? A well-engaged client is likely to stay on subject vs. a poorly engaged client will allow the topic of the session to meander to other apparently un-related topic areas. Again, look for changes in the client behaviour.

- Focus – Are you working on what the client wants to work on? Have you developed your own working hypothesis that is not that of the clients? Has your client allowed the original focus of the therapy to become lost? The measure here is whether or not you and your client are acknowledging and agreeing with these changes.

- Techniques and tools – is the client getting something useful out of the therapy? Are they looking for a more directive approach, or are they slowly tiring of your methods and lack of intervention? Perhaps your modality or training does not "permit" you to deploy different techniques – but are you prepared to talk openly and honestly about your capabilities and, if necessary, help that client find what they need? A periodic check-in with a client to ask them if they are finding the sessions useful might be all it takes to re-establish a confidence in you that keeps them engaged.

- Are there changes in payment patterns? Do they give me cash at the beginning of sessions? Are they "forgetful" or disorganised in making payments? Perhaps your clients are expressing resentment or passive-aggression in their patterns. Or maybe they are treating your services like any "service" transaction.
- Do I like this client? Do I feel lost with this client? Do I fancy this client?! Do I find myself thinking about this client outside of the therapy room? Maybe you're in touch with a transference or projection that you're reacting to – bring this counter-transferential reaction into consciousness will help you make better interventions and is a KPI to be measured – if you don't like your client, the risk is that this will be subtly visible and the relationship will suffer.

Client tracking form

In order to help you keep track of your client's presenting problem, session summaries, homework set (if that is part of your modality), attendance record and any other KPIs, we have developed a client tracking form in Appendix 4. (The notes written in are example notes from a fictitious client, and are there for your guidance).

Final words

We wish you well in developing your business. We hope that the material covered here has been, and will continue to be helpful to you. Be safe, be professional, be ethical. You can do it!

John Kennett & Jason Colyer.

Appendix 1 – Takings Journal

My Counselling Business | Week commencing: 9/9/13

Date	Client	Fee levied	Cash received	Cheques received	Transfers on account	Opening balance	Closing balance	Outstanding invoices	Due date
9/9/16	Frank T	£40.00				-£80.00	-£120.00	-£80.00	30/9/13
9/9/16	John B	£50.00	£50.00			£0.00	£0.00		
10/9/16	Bob J	£40.00		£160.00		£0.00	+£120.00		
	Steve S					-£120.00	-£120.00	-£80.00	30/9/13
10/9/16	Peter F	£40.00			£160.00	-£200.00	-£80.00	-£160.00	~~30/9/13~~
	Paula H					-£160.00	-£160.00	-£160.00	31/8/13
11/9/16	Jane Y	£50.00			£50.00	£0.00	£0.00		
11/9/16	Sue & Jon C	£60.00	£60.00			£0.00	£0.00		
	Turnover	Total cash	Total cheques	Total transfers			Total owed	Invoices outstanding	
	£280.00	£110.00	£160.00	£210.00			-£360.00	-£320.00	

Turnover prev. week	£3450.00
Turnover ytd	£3730.00

Banked this week	£110 + £160 = £270
Banked on date	11/9/13

Notes:

Quiet week due to me taking the weekend off.

Remember to chase Paula H – her invoice is overdue.

Appendix 2 – Example invoice

My Counselling Business
1, The Street
Township
County
AB1 2CD

INVOICE

Invoice # : 1706
Account # : 1703
Date : 1st July 2017

To: Mr D Duck
      The Avenue
      Over Yonder
      EF3 4GH

Date	Description	Fee	Balance
08/06/17	Session 15	£40.00	£40.00
15/06/17	Session 16	£40.00	£80.00
23/06/17	DNA	£40.00	£120.00
28/06/17	Session 17	£40.00	£160.00
		Total now due	£160.00

Please make cheques payable to **"Mrs A Therapist"**
and post to address above, or arrange electronic transfer to
Mrs A Therapist, account number 12345678, sort code 12-34-56

Please pay this months invoice by 31st July 2017

Please note that late payment incurs interest of 10% for each week overdue, and that we
reserve the right to recover unpaid amounts via debt collection agencies.

Appendix 3 – Statement of Account

My Counselling Business
1, The Street
Township
County
AB1 2CD

STATEMENT of
ACCOUNT

Account # : 1703
Date : 1ˢᵗ July 2017

To: Mr D Duck
        The Avenue
        Over Yonder
        EF3 4GH

Date	Description	Fee	Balance
08/06/17	Session 15	£40.00	£40.00
15/06/17	Session 16	£40.00	£80.00
23/06/17	DNA	£40.00	£120.00
28/06/17	Session 17	£40.00	£160.00
		Payments recieved	-£160.00
		Account balance	£0.00

Appendix 4 – Client tracking form

Client name / code :

Date	Session number	Punctuality (early, on-time, late, DNA, re-arranged)	Ending	Payment	On-topic engagement	Presenting Issue	Feelings towards this client	Feedback review	Last covered in super-vision

10610940R00081

Printed in Great Britain
by Amazon